The POWER
of CHOICE

The POWER
of CHOICE
Kelly Weekers

How to hack your happiness

English translation by Annoesjka Oostindiër

MOONSHOT PUBLISHING

MOONSHOT PUBLISHING B.V., Laren, The Netherlands.

MOONSHOT PUBLISHING 🚀

First published in the Netherlands by
Moonshot Publishing BV, 2022.
'The Power of Choice' is a translation of 'De Kracht van Keuze',
copyright © 2022 by Kelly Weekers.

Printed in The Netherlands.

For information: Moonshot Publishing, Oosterend 13,
1251 HM Laren, The Netherlands. Registered with the
Netherlands Chamber of Commerce under number 85922145.

Books in the Moonshot Publishing catalogue may be
purchased for educational or commercial use or for sales
promotions. For more information, please email:
support@moonshot-publishing.com.

Visit us online at moonshot-publishing.com.

ISBN 9789083260068

© 2022 Moonshot Publishing BV, The Netherlands
and Kelly Weekers.
English translation © 2022 Annoesjka Oostindiër.
Editing: Moonshot Publishing editorial team, assisted by
Joy Phillips.
Designed by Coco Bookmedia and Emma Peijnenburg.

For my girls.
The most beautiful thing you
can become is yourself.
Whatever path you two choose in life,
you have my unwavering support.

Love always, mom.

66

Whatever
the *situation*,
remind yourself
that you can
CHOOSE
how you want to
handle it.

99

CONTENTS

PREFACE

What shall I wear? What to eat for lunch? Go to work by car or take the bike? Change jobs or just stay where I am? Wait until my car's EMPTY light comes on or fill it up now? Work out or just chill on the couch? Wash my hair or hide the grease with dry shampoo? Renovate or move house? And if I move, then where to? Spend money on a vacation or save up? Meet a friend for drinks or opt for some me-time? Go out on the town or get up bright and early? Keep trying or split up? And what movie do I want to watch?

Whether it's trivial everyday matters or big life-changing decisions, sooner or later we all have to choose. And even though we often don't consciously think about all these insignificant choices, the big ones can trigger chronic stomach aches, stress and anxiety. They can also be a source of happiness, however. Whichever way you look at it, everyone on this planet has the power of choice, the power to decide how to deal with something that crosses their path.

I'd like to start off by saying that it took me quite a while to realize I actually had this power. Of course I made all sorts of decisions before that finally sank in. Not only regarding my studies, career, friendships, boyfriends and clothes, but also choices with regard to my thoughts, actions and words. In hindsight, I also made some 'bad' calls. Not that I regretted any of these decisions, it was more that I wasn't really making *my* choice. In fact, my choices were largely determined by what others told me to do, by my upbringing and by the choices people around me made. When I had to make a decision, I would usually not ask myself any questions beforehand, and if I did, they would be the wrong ones. So I didn't really think about what university major would make *me* happy, but whether my parents would be proud of me. I didn't ask myself which boyfriend would suit me, but whether we looked picture-perfect for the outside world. I didn't ask myself if I felt like going out; my friends wanted to, so I did. I didn't think about my outfit; the Spice Girls dressed like that, so I did as well. I either did things on autopilot, or I was more preoccupied with the opinions of others than with what *I* actually thought or wanted.

This insight only sunk in when I started studying

psychology; it was then that I discovered the power of choice. It was fascinating to learn so much about human beings, and therefore also about myself. To understand why people act the way they do. That's where I learned there's a space between stimulus and response, between action and reaction. It is that space that allows us to determine how we want to respond to something. Moreover, our response is largely determined by our beliefs. And those, in turn, are driven by our genes, upbringing, experiences and environment. The realization that I could adjust those dials was a huge eye-opener. What's more, I could even reset them. And while I had previously believed that I didn't have any options, or simply just didn't see they existed, all of a sudden they were becoming more visible and also so much more in line with my true self. More and more often I would ask myself: "Hey, wait a minute, what do *I* actually want?" That was the moment when I started to map out my own path.

I'm now at a point where the power of choice is a unifying theme running through my life. This has enabled me to distance myself from and leave behind all kinds of situations and people as well as parts of myself. By doing so, I have created more room for new experiences, for new people *and* for a nicer version of myself. Every day, it helps me deal in the best way possible – my *own* way – with the ups and downs that cross my path. What I cannot tell you in this book is which choices will work out best for you. What I *can* help you with, is understanding that you *always* have a choice. That there are often many more options than you might think. And by making choices true to your heart, they automatically become better choices, making your life more enjoyable and making you a happier person. By sharing my lessons and insights, I hope to help you reflect on your life. By giving you a glimpse of my thoughts and sharing how I went about it all, I hope you will start to believe that you can indeed choose your own path. That you are *allowed* to choose your own path. And that it's okay to change course when the old one no longer suits you. So let's go make some choices!

- Kelly

UPBRINGING

Personality-wise, I really am a good blend of my mom and dad. My dad is a 'cut the crap and get down to work' kind of guy. Without short-changing him, I think it's fair to say that he's a bit of a workaholic. I've definitely inherited this perfectionism of his, which can sometimes get a bit extreme, and I mean like *really* sinking my teeth into something for a *very* long time. But in my head I also hear my mother's voice say: "Alright now, time to take it easy, time for some fun!" I'm quite happy with that chameleon-like side of my character. At times I can be a bit pushy in what I want, but at other times I can just as easily loosen the reins.

This parental salt-and-pepper blend makes for a good balance. My dad is a bit quieter and calmer. In his heart of hearts he's not a social creature. That's something I can relate to; I love to withdraw to my own little corner of the world. I can be introvert and subdued, careful to maintain the balance between the hustle and bustle of everyday life and 'retreating into myself'. But just like my mother, I can also burst forth from my withdrawn mode into a state of high energy, whip out a bottle of wine and whoa, before you know it six hours of animated conversation and pondering over life's big questions have gone by. I once decided I wanted to try and capture my own personality, because I somehow thought I wasn't all that complicated. I hadn't exactly expected this collection of character traits:

I'm a totally down-to-earth kind of girl, but invariably dream big. I'm an introvert, but in the right company or if you let me yack about work, I won't stop talking. I make conscious choices, but often make decisions quickly, based on intuition. I have strong opinions about everything and everyone, but find people who are judgmental exhausting. I hate being away from my daughters, but enjoy the short spells when they're not around. I hate superficial stuff, but trash TV shows can make me as happy as a pig in the mud. I can revel in luxury, but simple things are what I enjoy most. I don't like to cook, but I absolutely love to eat. I'm not a control freak, but I prefer to do things myself. I love being alone, but am always available for 'my people'. I think it's dumb when people don't take their own talents seriously, but I also don't take people seriously if they're not able to laugh at themselves. I'm a real go-getter, but can put off something trivial like washing my hair for ages. I love sleeping, but also consider it a waste of time. Work is relaxation for me and doing nothing almost feels like work. I can make a big drama out of something trivial, but am great at trivializing something that actually *is* a big deal.

I'm a mishmash of my parents' genes and personalities. Having spent so much time with my grandparents when I was young, I also recognize their qualities in myself. I understand how the role models and lessons in my childhood, as well as those later on in life, have made me into the person I am today. I'm still far from being perfect, but I can truly say that I am myself. Reaching that point involved holding on as well as letting go. It is this journey I want to share with you, and it all starts with how I was raised.

*

I was born in the southern Dutch province of Limburg, in Weert, a town of about 50,000 people. Happiness was in the small things. My paternal grandparents opened a fashion store right after they were married. My parents later started their own fashion business. It took blood, sweat and tears; there was always so much to do and organize. I observed it all and learned from an early age that if I wanted something, I'd have to work for it. By that time, my grandparents had sold their store, and suddenly they, in contrast, had a lot of time on their hands. In kindergarten, I would stand in the school yard after class let out and stare down the road. Wasn't that their green Mercedes approaching? *XY-21-LY.* Nowadays, not a week goes by without me struggling to pay for parking because I've once again forgotten my license plate number, but my grandpa's is etched in my memory. *XY-21-LY.*

Since my parents were busy in the shop early every morning, Grandpa would come and pick me up to take me to school. Which was totally fine with me, because my grandparents spoiled me with attention and love. "What do you want to eat, Kel? What would you like?" And poof, they would whip up some apple pancakes for me. After I'd cleaned my plate: "How about a jigsaw puzzle together?" Or we'd go on outings! Hiking in the forest and learning about nature, or visiting a town, armed with a book about its history. My grandparents and I also often went on road trips. They had a small camping trailer in which we toured the whole country, from south to north and from east to west. But we also went to Rome, including Vatican City, and were always on the lookout for art, culture and nature. The world was really opened up to me, and my grandparents taught me something very important: that you have to really *want* life. And to just *do* things. Work hard, play hard. That's a lesson I made sure not to forget.

My maternal grandparents had a pig farm. Oh, how I loved being there! It was a dream come true for a little girl like me. It didn't matter if it was sunny, rainy, hailing, warm, cold or thundering, my cousins and I would always be outside. My imagination ran wild while I played dress-up, spread out pillows on the barn floor, rolled around in the mud and got all dirty. We built huts, played in the cornfield and leaped over ditches. Back indoors, with a cup of hot chocolate, we would listen to stories about the Second World War with bated breath. "Grandma, please tell us again about that bridge that was bombed and about having to cross the water over a narrow board." It struck me that she would never complain about the war, nor about life in general. She was also a great storyteller, as if the war had been a novel. She never focused on the awful aspects and always stressed the few opportunities that she *did* still have and that she *was* able to grasp. She knew about poverty and war, lost her husband at a young age, and worked tirelessly. Mind you, Grandma had plenty of reasons to complain. I don't think I realized it back then, but later on it struck me that this was a choice she made. You can either label your fate as challenging and difficult, or focus on the good things instead, however dark it might have been or sometimes still is. Grandma was always cheerful and positive, a born optimist.

When I got a bit older, we would hop on our bikes after school and cycle five miles to the farm, over small country lanes, straight across the pastures. It was a carefree time. Cell phones didn't exist yet, so we didn't have to constantly let others know where we were, and we always arrived safely. Looking at pictures from that era, it strikes me that I'm always outside and all dirty, either on a campsite or in muddy wellies on the farm.

My grandpa died when I was three. He had cancer and died just six weeks after the diagnosis. We visited his grave often, and even though I was still very young his death marked the first big moment in my life. All of a sudden he wasn't there anymore and Grandma Liesje 'became the farm'. I vividly remember how her kitchen smelled. And her soup, with all the leftovers that went right back in the pot. The next day, the same pot of soup would appear on the table. I have to admit this is probably also the root cause of my germaphobia, but mostly a source of happiness. We had very little in those days, but it was still a lot, and it was enough. I was a happy child.

*

For six years I was the only child, until my sister Romy was born. Wow! Love at first sight. People sometimes say it can be difficult when you've been the darling of the family for years and ta-da! you suddenly have a sibling. They say children can become jealous, since they're no longer unique. I've never felt that, never experienced it like that. On the contrary, suddenly I had everything I'd ever dreamed of. A sister!

What about my parents' love for me and my sister? It was unconditional. Not that they would talk about it, because expressing their feelings wasn't really their thing. But it was obvious; their actions, glances and gestures were brimming with love. At home emotions were handled in a stoical, 'Limburgian' manner – typical for the region where we lived. In a nutshell, we were all expected to avoid becoming too emotional and to just act normal, without any fuss or drama. My parents couldn't handle 'too emotional'. In fact, in our family we still don't go in for "complicated" either, believing that makes no sense and is a waste of time. At home, the phrase "everything will be fine!" was a classic. And that was it, that's how every problem was nipped in the bud. I was used to a loving and supportive home. It was never clingy; none of us liked clingy. Nor did we like difficult conversations. Extreme highs and lows simply didn't seem to occur around me. Life just kind of happened and there were always people who had it harder than I did – come on, chin up!

I think Grandpa was one of the few people around me who was comfortable being emotional. I have a very clear memory of the time when we were watching a popular Dutch feel-good TV show together. Out of the corner of my eye, I saw tears rolling down his cheeks. I was pretty young then and asked: "Why are you crying, Grandpa?" "Because I'm so happy for them, sweetie." Tears of joy! Wow, I'd never seen those before!

The six years' age difference between me and my sister was significant. For six years, I was the king of the castle and everything revolved around me. I knew my parents worked hard to give us a good life and I could see their efforts were paying off because we could afford more and more things. I did my best to do my part as well by being overly diligent. It took little effort; that was just who I was, a sweet and industrious busy bee. I was also extremely concerned about others and did my best to try and conform to their expectations. A true child of Limburg, I was raised with the ever-present thought, "Oh dear, imagine what other people might think!" Well, in that case better make sure they thought the right thing. I was very adept at that. I was both shy and perfectionistic, a guarantee for peace and cleanliness. "What a perfect child, no need to worry about her. Kel can take care of herself," I would often overhear my parents say. And so that's exactly what I did.

That didn't change with my sister's arrival. My mother had by then cut back on work hours, but of course the baby still needed to be fed, bathed and dressed, and I wanted a front-row seat. Within a few years, I was the one who took Romy to school on the back of my bike, often cycling all the way to Grandma's farm. Did she want a sandwich or some fruit? Did she want to play along with me and my friends? Borrow my clothes or make-up, only to never give it back? I was a child who was fine with everything and enjoyed taking care of others. "Let Kel be a child, she's such a serious girl." I can still hear my aunt saying that. But I'd be off again and go right on doing what I thought everyone expected of me. I didn't mind; that role fit me like a glove.

My childhood flew by and I was lucky that I was smart, even though I never aimed for straight As. Besides, a B or B minus was enough to pass to the next grade. Pretty soon I started applying my perfectionism selectively to choose what I wanted to spend time on. Only when something felt very good

– a specific subject at school, for instance – would I seriously put in the time to do my best.

But what *really* made me happy was work. I was allowed to help out in the shop from a young age. There we'd all be, surrounded by boxes full of buttons, boxes full of buckles, boxes full of scarves. Oh, the smell of glue and leather... Everything in my parents' shop was made by hand. That world of fashion is where I grew up and soon I became part of the team. In would come a lady with a blazer, asking if we happened to have a cognac-colored button that matched the fabric perfectly. And which belt should go with that? And there I'd be, ten years old and frantically, excitedly searching for just the right thing in the haberdashery store once established by my grandparents, which by then had been taken over by my aunt.

As a child, I loved being one of the grownups. The fact that they involved me felt incredibly good. *Yes! Together we've got this!* That experience brought me so much. In our family it was also totally normal to help out. Lending a hand in the shop and earning some pocket money was great. The older I was, the more I was allowed to do, and I got more and more skilled at it too. I babysat my cousins, ran the take-out counter at the local Chinese restaurant, mixed drinks behind the bar, and then a bit later on, started walking the catwalk! There was nothing to it; modeling was easy and I wanted to be the best at everything I did. All the money I earned went into a savings account, because that's another thing that had been ingrained in me, to be frugal with money. After all, there had been a time when we couldn't afford to spend much at all, and who knows what could happen...

I knew my parents were proud of my work ethic and responsible behavior. And that didn't change once I was a teenager. No need to tell me what time I had to be home, nor which friends I could hang out with; things just automatically went smoothly. I had a close-knit circle of friends; we had a lot of fun together and supported each other. Sure, sometimes I would have a bit too much to drink, but drugs or smoking? No, thank you. And since I was always a wreck after a night of drinking – this is still the case by the way – I never went beyond that one night. My teenage rebellion was limited to occasionally hanging over the toilet bowl, a fling with a boss who was much older. That was it.

My parents and grandparents tirelessly taught me to show initiative, to enjoy life and do things. Don't sit around and wait for things to happen, but embrace life. "You've got to do things, Kel, *do* things." And no, I wasn't smothered with displays of affection, in the sense of putting an arm around me or hugging me tight. But I've always felt the affection and emotions that they may have been unable to show openly. I was cherished and hugged with words, actions, glances and quality time. My childhood, both at home and when I was at my grandparents', gave me something of infinite value: a safe and loving environment.

66

Change what
you can change.
accept and LET
GO of what you
cannot change.

99

At the age of 18, I spread my wings and went to college in Maastricht, the capital of the province where we lived. The active part of my upbringing was complete, but of course I brought along my experiences and many of the beliefs I had been raised with. It was only later that the impact of my upbringing on the choices I made became clear to me. I come from a close, warm family. We were and are still always and unconditionally there for one another. Even nowadays, I talk to my parents and sister on a daily basis and we hang out together every week or so – and with any luck, four (!) generations are present. When I look back on the first eighteen years of my life, I thank my lucky stars. It was so much more than just 'good'. There were no big dramas, at least not that I remember. If there was some sort of problem, we quickly put things in their proper perspective and carried on. Being level-headed, having a sense of perspective and a positive outlook, stability, a good work ethic, a close-knit family that cares for each other and is there for one another – what a great combination of characteristics to enter adulthood with.

Of course I've experienced more since then and learned a lot of other things, but I don't consider those very relevant. Trying to come up with a comprehensive list would only mean getting bogged down in details. Besides, the childhood I just described also included a hefty dose of self-mockery and sarcasm to ensure you didn't start thinking you were oh-so-important or would want to tell others your oh-so-detailed, terribly boring life story in book form.

What I want to emphasize is that your roots always soak into you. Whether your childhood was quiet or intense or everything in between, it shapes you. That's not a bad thing; it makes sense and can be great. But it's good to become aware of those tendencies and patterns in yourself, and to realize you have a choice. What do you want to take with you into the future and what would you rather leave behind? It's extra important when you've had to deal with serious shit as a kid. Just because a certain strategy worked when you were small doesn't mean it's still the best way to think or behave. You might want other things from life now – and that means you'll probably have to start doing things differently too!

I have cherished this down-to-earth attitude for quite a while and am still Miss No-Nonsense. But you can overdo it. Sure, it has its advantages, but at some point what I considered to be my small-town mindset started to annoy me. Because yes, being down-to-earth and 'normal' is good, but at the same time it made me overly concerned about other people's possible opinions and judgments. It's not like the "just be normal and act normal" attitude is particularly nice for yourself. No, it's all about the outside world and about what other people think. Yes indeed, what are they thinking?! I spent way too many years letting other people's opinions determine my choices. And if there is such a thing as a recipe for unhappiness, that would be it. If there's anything that will lead to bad decision-making, it's letting your actions be guided by what others might think about your choices.

These days, I ask myself a much better question: "Does it matter what others might or might not be thinking? In the end what counts is what *I* think, right?" The question should be: "Will it make *me* happy? Will it make the people that really matter to me happy?" Being down-to-earth is a great asset, absolutely, but it should no longer be instrumental in keeping you small. I really like people that are down-to-earth and just 'act normal', but if you don't feel like just acting normal, that's totally fine too. Because what is 'normal' after all? Normal is different for every individual. In my case, holding on to that belief from the past was holding me back and interfering with what I wanted to get out of life. So I tried to figure out the right balance that worked for me.

But feeling so responsible is still tricky at times. I'm not a risk taker and I definitely don't have a self-destructive side. But sometimes it feels so good to be able to cut myself some slack without having to juggle everything. To briefly let myself relax without telling myself I need to make good use of my time. To briefly enjoy taking care of myself instead of having to take care of others; that it's time for some much-needed self-care. To feel young. To avoid having a midlife crisis, because you may suddenly start thinking you've missed out on a lot of things when you reach 45.

All my life, I've heard that I'm so mature for my age, but are you born as an adult or does the outside world make you grow up fast? Hard to say. What I *do* know is that until recently I felt like I had to do everything myself and thought it was a sign of weakness if I took a break or asked for help. And yes, of course I am perfectly capable of doing everything myself, but being able to ask for help can feel so good. By not asking for help, I have often made things unnecessarily difficult for myself. I still do that sometimes, because that's just embedded in who I am. In a way, it is also about emotional development, and I might have fallen a bit short in that department. On the plus side, it meant that I didn't have much trouble with ups and downs, although it also made me somewhat of an emotional flatliner. Really enjoying myself, in the sense of jumping for joy, did not come easy to me. And when I *was* sad or stressed, I could be very hard on myself. "Don't be such a wuss. Come on, you can do this! Things could be a lot worse, Kel."

I am still far from moody but am so much more connected to my feelings now. Yes, things could be a lot worse, but that doesn't mean you can't feel bad when you're in the middle of it. I am kinder to myself in the sense that I finally allow myself to feel a bit low sometimes. I know my feelings are valid and don't tell myself to toughen up anymore. I now know that being a sniveling wreck or feeling angry every so often is okay. And that's such a relief. I am only now realizing that people who always think they have to be strong are in fact quite vulnerable. Vulnerability is actually a sign of strength. I'm not ashamed of anything anymore, and that is precisely why I feel so strong.

But suppose you learned or experienced very different things growing up. Heavy stuff. Like emotional overload. Explosive anger. Sadness, aggression, fear, insecurity and uncertainty. Patterns you yourself start to repeat – or perhaps you turn to your familiar coping mechanism to avoid the problem, which is unhelpful in the long run.

If you want to start choosing your own happiness, it's important to balance out those personality traits and patterns from your childhood. What do you really want to take with you? What do you want to downscale? And what do you want to get rid of altogether? Are there other things you might have missed out on that you'd like to add? Labeling your childhood as either good or bad isn't going to make you happy. What really helped me going forward is determining what I liked and wanted to keep, and what I wanted to change or let go of completely.

It doesn't make sense to hang on to something you had too much or too little of. Regardless, the past is the past. You can't change it anymore, so spending all your energy on it is only going to cause stress. We can only make a difference in the present and in the future. Your childhood, or rather, approximately all the years until your eighteenth birthday – the cutoff point that I chose to use in this book for the sake of convenience – is a defining period in your life.

Questions that have helped me choose the path of happiness include: What do I miss most from my childhood? How can I reclaim those things and pass them on? What advice would I give my younger self and would I want to make sure my older inner child hears? What do I personally want to take with me? So far I have solely focused on the impact on you as an individual, but of course it also affects the way you react to your family and friends. How do you want to deal with that? Which people do you want along for the ride? What do you want to take with you as a parent? And in romantic relationships? In friendships? It might all sound a bit complicated right now, but I want to try and make it as simple as possible for you to stay true to yourself, to walk *your* path and keep heading in your chosen direction. But first, let's take a closer look at the concept of mindsets.

"

LETTING GO
does not always mean
that you can *end*
something in the way
you envisioned it, but
that you feel that you are
NEVERTHELESS worthy
of a *new* beginning.

"

MINDSET

As soon as we wake up, we start making choices. We choose to have a sandwich or eat yogurt for breakfast. We choose to wear a skirt or pants. We choose to reply to a message right away, or not. Some of our choices are a little more complicated, of course. We choose our friends. We choose how we let others treat us. We choose to stay in a relationship rather than leave. We choose to focus either on abundance or on what's lacking. We choose to have a positive or negative outlook on life. We choose to hold on or to let go. To feel gratitude or jealousy. From the smallest actions to the biggest decisions, all day long you're making all kinds of choices, consciously or otherwise. Your brain mostly does this on autopilot, which is a good thing when you think of how many choices you make every day. You could get a burnout from less.

I can't tell you how happy it makes me to be in control and to realize that I am the one who makes these choices. To know that when someone offends me or says something negative, I can choose to feel hurt or sad and whether I want to react or just let it go. When I'm tired, I am the one who can choose to carry on, or ask for help and let myself get some rest. When I drop something on the floor and it breaks, or when I forget something, it is *my* choice if I'm going to feel bad about that and for how long. How people treat me is also my choice. *I* am the one who's in control, not other people or 'life in general'.

It might sound simple to be able to make choices and take the wheel all the time, but I've noticed it can be quite difficult. Because here's the thing: your values influence your decisions and the whole process goes very quickly and automatically. *Bam!* You've already reacted and will have to deal with the consequences, since you didn't really feel you even had a choice. And once you've finally made a choice, it's sometimes more like, "Wait, why the fuck am I doing this?!" I've discovered there are two crucial steps if you want to reap the benefits of the power of choice in your life:

1. *Realize you have a choice.*
2. *Make the right choice by asking yourself the right questions.*

*

I'm sure everyone feels stuck in life at some point: stuck in a relationship, in work, or in a friendship, or bogged down by health issues or grief. You might start thinking: It's no use, it won't change, it is what it is. Yet you can choose to do something about it. Or choose not to. You might now say: "Yeah right, saying goodbye is easier said than done, that bitch is family!" I get that and I hear lots of people saying similar things, but that doesn't make it true. Kudos to my parents for always giving me the idea I had options. Which didn't mean the options themselves were always great. Sometimes it meant having to work harder and earn less for a while. (But it would also mean that I was done with that shitty job and could still make a living.) Sometimes it meant a difficult conversation. (Breaking up with someone because I was no longer happy in a relationship, even though I also hate hurting others.) Or I had to apologize to a friend. (I hadn't really been there for her.)

But I did have options. I had the feeling I was in charge. Sometimes I had to overcome obstacles to get where I wanted to be. Fact is, when you think you don't have a choice, you keep on doing the same thing over and over. If you believe you don't have a choice, you feel trapped. Believing in choices will create opportunities. Instead of thinking, "I don't have any choices," go and fetch paper and a pen and sit down to think about what choices you *do* have. Think as hard as you can and as long as it takes until you have a fairly long list. Once again, your options won't always be great, but they do exist. The more you look for solutions, the more you will find them.

It's also true that although you can make choices in life, that doesn't necessarily mean everything is feasible. At times something comes your way and you won't be able to do anything about it. "Everything happens for a reason" is what some people would say to that. To which I would answer: "Bullshit, awful things happen all the time! It's just plain bad luck!" At some time in our lives, we all have to deal with unpleasant situations we wouldn't choose ourselves. Some people encountered those situations in childhood, others after reaching adulthood. For some people it's relationships, and for others it's their health. But whatever it is, you will somehow have to find a way to deal with it.

The question is what works best for you. What would be the best solution in your case? The fact that it's not your fault, that you don't deserve it and didn't want this, won't make it go away. Does it help to pitch your tent in Camp Self-Pity, whine until you are blue in the face, and resign yourself to the fact that you are doomed? Or would it be better to figure out how to make sure you can take the reins again? To look for possibilities and options? To think about what lessons it can bring you? Yes, life isn't always nice, but we do have the choice to try and make it as nice as possible.

I've noticed that in life lots of things take a turn for the better once people take matters into their own hands and dare to make changes. When two people face exactly the same situation, the one with the most positive mindset has a better chance to get through it and overcome it. A positive mindset makes a big difference and means that we won't get paralyzed – and more importantly, we'll feel more in charge of things. If we always have the feeling things 'just happen' to us, we run the risk of becoming apathetic. It's all too easy to feel we're stuck in a situation. To think: W*hy is this happening to me?* Negative emotions and difficulties are bound to happen, they're normal. I'd even say 'good'. My motto? Tackle it head-on instead of avoiding it. And yes, it's okay to indulge yourself and snuggle up under a blanket on the couch with a pint of ice cream and have a good cry. But it is also up to you to get up again and not still be sitting there a month later. It's a choice to not get stuck in that kind of mindset. And that creates room for growth. It means that instead of feeling miserable, you get a sense of purpose and see it as a life lesson.

I've always taken responsibility for how I deal with things that came my way. Because you know what? If I believed that I didn't have a choice, I'd be someone who remains incapable of changing anything about my own circumstances. As soon as I acknowledge that my life is my own and that everything that happens to me – whether it's my fault or not – is my responsibility, a shift takes place. Then I am no longer a victim of circumstance, but become master of the circumstances. It means I can be pro-active and push things in the direction I want them to go in. It means my life will shape itself more and more into how I would like it to be, because I'm actively working towards that and don't wait until something or someone else makes things right.

*

To reiterate, what is the power of choice for me personally? It's realizing that you can choose how to deal with issues, and then choosing what is best for you. I have always known that I had a choice in how to tackle things that cross my path. And that's not only because I was in luck in terms of DNA but also because I saw people around me doing it that way.

That's just how I was raised and what I saw family and friends doing.

My problem was that I let myself be guided by the wrong questions and therefore wasn't happy. I always wondered what others would think about my decisions. Had I maybe offended someone? Did people still like me? And did they agree I was doing 'the right thing'? I was primarily focused on and concerned with what I *thought* other people expected of me when making a choice, instead of taking my own happiness into account. It took a while before that sunk in; I had no idea it was my 'default setting'. Getting to know yourself and making more choices with your own happiness in mind is a journey everyone has to make in life. What do you *really* want from life? How do you want to live your life? I have a pretty clear idea of that at this point, but I'm guessing that every new phase and life-changing event will probably be accompanied by a slight shift in priorities. Since I now know the trick, I would like to share it with you, so that you too can continue to make choices with your happiness in mind.

Looking at the person you are today, what and who shaped you? After all, babies aren't born as a blank slate. First of all there's your DNA – the genetic factors – your factory settings, as it were. On top of that comes a big dollop of education and all kinds of life experiences. Who are you deep down inside? I sometimes no longer know what's nature and what's nurture, but I've also learned it is smarter to not let that matter. There are times when it's obvious: "Aha! That's absolutely due to my grandmother's genes." Or: "Wait a minute, I finally understand why I do that! Because of that event in the past that had such an impact on me." At other times it's difficult to put your finger on it. Sometimes we simply don't know why we do what we do. Luckily, we don't necessarily have to know everything. But what you *do* want to determine is the extent to which you want to take certain elements with you on your journey, regardless of where they came from. Ask yourself what you would like to change about yourself. What do you want to change about your surroundings? What do you want to take along with you, and what is no longer welcome in your life and would you consequently rather leave behind?

Self-insight and self-awareness are crucial for making the changes you want. That level of understanding helps you discern which choices are needed to make your life better and more fun. You might realize you have to address a particular personal issue in your love life or your friendships. Or maybe a career change is in order? You could discover you don't want to change anything just yet, because you're not quite ready for it, or because you have come to the conclusion that changing things right now isn't *that* important after all. "Oh, never mind," you might find yourself thinking. In that case, please don't bother spending time and energy on it. Why keep on complaining or feeling stuck about things you're not going to change anyway?

Deciding *not* to make a choice is also a choice. In that case you're choosing to accept something for what it is. And there's nothing wrong with that – but do stick to your decision, please. You can keep bitching about a friendship for ages, but if you don't sit down for a good talk or say goodbye to that friend, nothing is going to change. You can keep kvetching about your job, but if you're not going to ask for a raise or look for other job openings, things will remain the way they've always been. Accept it and move on! Fun fact: ultimately, no one can avoid making choices altogether, because we're *always* making decisions. Sometimes we choose change, at other times acceptance.

66

It is important
to *choose* for YOURSELF.
Regardless of whether
it will receive the
APPROVAL of the rest
of the world or not.
This is YOUR LIFE.
And *only* you know what
works best for you.

99

Self-reflection is important for making better choices. I reflected on the way I was raised, for instance, but also on my relationships with both friends and lovers, on motherhood, on my ambitions and on many other things I'd like to share with you in this book. By getting to know myself better and figuring out why I behave the way I do, I discovered what was preventing me from making better decisions. Because here's the thing: you do have to start by identifying what you want. Or rather, you have to know what you want and what you don't, even if this has changed over time. And to be able to figure that out, it is helpful to take a time-out whenever a particular situation or person causes tension. Take a step back and figure out what that tension is trying to tell you.

1. *Why is this situation making me feel uncomfortable?*
2. *What would I prefer instead?*
3. *What can I do to get closer to that goal?*

Coping with life's challenges is much easier when you know yourself and know what your values are. One of my tricks is to make a point of stepping out of the emotion and the situation; I look at the bigger picture. I ask myself: "Why am I feeling uncomfortable? What kind of situation am I dealing with? What thoughts does it trigger? And what emotions?" If you're like most people, you will want to react quickly. *Bam!* Animalistically, acting purely on instinct – due to the combination of genes, upbringing and life experiences. When someone makes a nasty remark, people generally want to respond right away. When we see a picture-perfect photo online, we immediately start questioning whether we're happy with our own life. When someone asks us or offers us something, our first reaction is to think we have to say yes or no straight away. This holds true even when the smarter choice would be to think about it for a while, to distance yourself from it and then very consciously determine what it is you want and how you'd prefer to react. Taking a little break amidst all the action and reaction does wonders for your life. So remember: action – pause – reaction.

You can teach yourself to create space for conscious choices. And please know that you can and are in fact *allowed* to say: "I'll get back to you about that." Or: "Let me think about that for a while." Ask yourself: "What do I *really* want?" Don't say yes or no immediately, but postpone your response. Give yourself some time and space to choose more consciously and intentionally. In our world of sensory overload, zooming out is a great tool. It creates space to make your own happiness more of a priority, since your inner authentic voice becomes so much clearer and louder. It amplifies the voice that corresponds to who you want to be and what you want to get out of life, instead of the person you once were – or thought you were.

*

There is only one certainty in life, and that is death. All the rest is a nice extra. And yes, I know that's a wry way of putting it. Our choices largely determine the quality of the journey and how enjoyable it will be. Using the power of choice at defining moments is a crucial part of moving forward in life and steering it in a more joyful direction.

I use this power when I'm not crazy about something. Or when something costs me too much energy. Or when I'd prefer a different alternative. Whenever that happens, I'm so glad I actually have the power to change things. While it started with something simple as daring to say, "I don't feel like it, so I'm not going out with you guys tonight," it evolved into much more important choices regarding friendships, love and life in general.

I'm also done with that whole paradox of choice thing, weighing up the pros and cons, endlessly pondering and procrastinating. As a perfectionist,

I've done more than my share of deliberation. Because in the end that is what perfectionism boils down to: it's hidden insecurity – and that applies to me as well. Being afraid of what other people might think of a decision. Being afraid of other people judging me, but also fearing my own critical inner voice, berating myself for making a 'mistake'. And the fear of failure, of course.

By now, I have grasped that there are always millions of options and we can never be certain which one is best. I've learned to let go of the urge to try and make the perfect choice. So instead I now ask myself, "What would I choose once I'm able let go of all my fears?" That's the choice I make, and then I just wait and see what happens. Because I've also discovered that as long as it isn't a life-or-death issue, every door that closes does indeed open hundreds of others. As long as I choose with the right intentions, I have nothing to worry about. And as long as I choose x or y because I think it will make me happier, I'd say that's a pretty good inner compass.

I deliberately chose to leave the bad stuff behind because I wanted better for myself. But I've also said goodbye to good things because I wanted *more*. In love, for instance, but I will tell you more about that later. And sure, it can be scary, but you gain so much by making up your mind. I've learned it's okay to make mistakes. And that it makes no sense to be hard on myself when that happens. As long as I don't let the opinions of others become too important, there's really not a lot to worry about. Please remember the following as a general rule: as long as it's not a matter of life or death, I'd say you're doing fine. As long as it's nothing major like "I might not live to tell the tale", in most cases I would recommend that you go for it. Maybe you're reading this and thinking: "Hm, isn't that a bit over the top?" Actually, no. In my view, the inordinate amount of time we humans spend thinking about all sorts of stupid things is over the top and completely ridiculous. Things that you will give exactly zero fucks about a year from now. Like: "Oh, do I look good enough on the picture that I'm about to post online... Maybe I should choose a different one?" and then turning that into a lengthy 'worry marathon' and wasting a whole evening. Come on, who cares!? And hey, why do we even have to take all kinds of insignificant people and factors into account when making a decision? Sure, you can choose to worry about those things. But you can also decide that you no longer want to be bothered with that. I've stopped caring about those kinds of things. We shouldn't take life for granted; sickness and loss made me realize that. My time is too precious. I've chosen to make things as nice as possible for myself, and I aim to keep it that way. So let's go and put these principles into practice!

*

And no, I'm not saying this so that you can sit down at the kitchen table with your partner and say: "Listen, I've read Kelly's book and I've decided I want to choose happiness for myself. I want a divorce and I'm quitting my job. Oh and by the way, I'm also taking the kids and moving to the other side of the world." Noooooooooooooooo! Please don't do that. Important choices should be given careful thought; they should be conscious decisions. But I *would* like you to become aware of the fact that you have options. More accurately, what I'd really like is for you to have a shift in mindset. Shifting from, "I'm trapped; there is no other way; this is just how it is," to "Hey, wait a minute, I *do* have options and I'm in charge here." And if you decide to leave things the way they are, that's your choice as well. Don't get me wrong, it's not like I'm constantly maximizing my choices; good is often good enough. That's part of the reason why I'm so laid back about things. But that too is about being in control, and just that feeling alone, that you're running the show, will already make you so much happier.

However, often things are not fine the way they are. In that case, doing nothing only because you're afraid you might be making the wrong choice could mean getting stuck in that situation for years. You could become a very bitter person. Take it from me: no one besides you can turn things around. Be the hero in your own life! As soon as you start believing you have options and dare to choose what you really want, you've already taken the most important step towards change. In most cases, that will vastly improve your life.

But what if you really hate your job or are in a bad relationship? Then my advice is to get out of there. Dare to say to yourself: "I have no idea what's on the other side of the mountain, but this here, right now, is not right for me." There are tons of people who are unhappy because of work, friendships, relationships or something inside themselves. Well then, go and do something about it! And do it regardless of the outcome, because no one can ever know that beforehand. Do it regardless of what other people might think, because you can never please everyone. Get moving and choose already! The key to happiness is understanding that how you want to deal with something is *always* your choice – however shitty the situation is. Even if it means having to deal with an unwanted situation. Even if you have to make minor changes later because your decision turns out less well than expected. Scientific research has proven time and again – and I've experienced this in my own life many, many times – that the simple fact of taking the wheel will make you a happier person, regardless of the outcome.

*

When I was studying psychology at university, I learned something very important about the power of choice from the German psychiatrist Viktor Frankl. He was a prisoner in a concentration camp in Nazi Germany during the Second World War, survived the Holocaust and later wrote a poignant book about it: *A Man's Search for Meaning*. I would like to quote him here: "Everything can be taken from a man, but one thing: the last of the human freedoms – to choose one's attitude in any given set of circumstances, to choose one's own way." His ideas about dealing with his dreadful situation made a huge impression on me. Even when life gives us the very worst, we retain the freedom to choose how to deal with it. Even in the deepest and darkest moments of our lives, we still have a choice how we want to frame a situation and respond to it. Well, if someone in a concentration camp is able to do that, who am I to think I might have a valid excuse for imagining I don't have any alternatives?

Bibian Mentel, the Dutch Olympic snowboarding star, is another role model of mine, someone who clearly decided: I'm not going to leave it at this, I might be very sick, but I want to exercise as much control as possible. That choice did not make the cancer go away and she did eventually die of the disease, but in the meantime she excelled, enjoyed life, created things and inspired and helped loads of people. Because of her enormous resilience, she was able to give an incredibly powerful and special meaning to all those years of illness. What I really admire about her was how she was able to accept all the problems she faced – which were far from minor. She kept on dreaming big dreams; she wanted to participate in the Olympics and succeeded over and over. She aimed for the stars, and reached them. Her achievements gave her and the people around her a solid foundation of joy, anticipation and hope. She kept on finding new long-term goals to aim for; that gave her a certain drive. She continued walking her own path, even though she was forced to take very unwelcome side roads. She continued doing things her way and was the master of her own life. I think that's incredibly admirable! She inspired me; she gave me a sort of kick in the pants to get my act together. In my life I've been spoiled by fate, but it reminded me that I should keep on choosing, keep having the courage to take new steps and make use of the fact that I have the luxury of choice.

It is my impression that people who harness the power of choice are often the happiest, even when they face dire circumstances. Viktor Frankl, Bibian Mentel, as well as many other people I personally know and certain things that happened around me – but more about that later – it made me realize that life isn't fair and that we may not be able to control everything. Even so, we still have a lot to choose in all those things we *do* control. It's wonderfully liberating to become aware of the fact that we always have the choice to deal with matters in our own way. It means you can – to a large extent – choose how to direct the course of your life and how joyful that life journey turns out to be.

66

The world around us
is nothing more than a
reflection of who we are.
CHANGE your mindset,
change your world.

99

SELF-ESTEEM

When I moved out to go to college, I wanted to go to the big city. *Maastricht, here I come!* I had a high school diploma in my pocket and was ready for the next step. I really looked forward to studying and student life. Well uh, oops... I kind of messed that up, because in the beginning my attitude was more like: *Oh yeah, I'm actually here to study, right!?* Part of the reason was that I'd made the wrong choice. When I enrolled, I wasn't sure what I wanted to major in. Law or psychology? Psychology had been a personal interest of mine for years. But yeah, there we go again... I chose to go to law school. Not because it particularly appealed to me, but because I thought a law degree would make others have a higher opinion of me. In those days, studying psychology was not taken seriously by everyone. It might sound ridiculous now, but back then, in 2007, self-development was for loonies and clinical psychologists were assumed to be working with 'madmen'. Some people probably even thought that people who majored in psychology were a bit crazy themselves and maybe primarily did it as self-study.

High school was a breeze. I did absolutely zilch for weeks on end, just showed up in class but didn't study at all, and then at the last moment, after a couple of nights of cramming for an exam, *ta-da!* I'd pass. Let me briefly explain that getting straight As wasn't important to me at all. Like many high school students in the Netherlands, I did the bare minimum required and knew exactly how to go about that. But as a law student, I couldn't get away with that anymore. The first midterm exams were a disaster. My usual steady Cs suddenly dropped to Ds. And the lectures were so incredibly boring that I'd sometimes fall asleep. At the end of my freshman year, I didn't have enough credits and was kicked out. In the end, I finally did decide to switch my major to psychology and neuroscience, subjects much more to my liking, and things turned out fine. It triggered my inquisitive side and I found fresh motivation not just to go to bars, but also to show up in class. As soon as something grabs my attention, I want to know absolutely everything about it – but when something bores me, I sit back and zone out.

It was around that time that I read an article in

the paper that the Miss Netherlands pageant was in danger of becoming a Miss Western Holland pageant. They had received very few applications from girls from the more rural provinces elsewhere in the country. As someone from one of those provinces – Limburg is in the south-east of the Netherlands – the story caught my eye. I was especially intrigued because I'd already been modeling on the side for a few years; it was more fun than delivering newspapers and certainly paid much better. So giving the national pageant a try seemed like a good opportunity to get more modeling work.

I applied without really knowing what it entailed and had to put in an appearance three weeks later. I went there in sneakers and jeans, and by late afternoon I was crowned Miss Limburg, including the whole fancy get-up with the sash and crown. I'd always been a bit of a tomboy, so I felt a bit like a circus animal in a prom dress. But all right, fine, I put on the sash and posed for a picture… And then they said: "Now you can also compete in the national Miss Netherlands pageant. And if you win that, you could become Miss Universe and go to the number one pageant in the world. That's where every single girl wants to go to."

I didn't have a clue what I was getting into, but it sounded fun, so I thought, "Okay, let's go for it!" Long story short, I actually became Miss Netherlands, and I also made it to the final round of Miss Universe in Brazil; I was the first Dutch girl in twenty years to get that far. The modeling agency I had been working for advised me to take a year off and become a fulltime model. That would allow me to move abroad and get more jobs instead of having to say: "Oh sorry, that date is not going to work out, because I have classes or an exam." I had just finished my bachelor's degree in psychology and neuroscience and thought, "All right, I'll take a sabbatical and do it for a year. That way, later on, I will never have any regrets and wonder 'if only I had tried'."

But it didn't work out that way, because I almost immediately got really homesick. I traveled from Brazil to Turkey, Germany, the USA and then onwards to Italy, but all I could think about was everything I was missing – my family, friends, the parties, the cozy conviviality back home. I found out I was a born homebody, and now I was suddenly thrust into a very strange setting that required me to be thin, beautiful and silent all the time. In those days, keeping your mouth shut was really a thing in the modeling scene. They weren't looking for models with a personality; all that counted was having the right looks and sizes. I got nasty remarks about the way I looked every single day. It had a huge impact on me, because I started believing those negative voices. The opinions of others became way too important; in my eyes they became the truth. I started thinking about things I had never thought about before, like believing my hips were too wide and my face wasn't symmetrical. I became insecure. Was it okay to eat this, was I allowed to do that, why wasn't I good enough as I was? I started comparing myself to the other girls, who, in my opinion, were doing better than me and were more beautiful and more successful. And soon my life revolved around posing, working out and strictly eating salads only. And all the while other people kept telling me: "Oh wow, Kel! You get to travel all over the world and live in all kinds of fantastic places! That's so cool!" Well, to be honest, I didn't think it was everything it was cracked up to be. Almost every day, I thought, "jeez, Kel, what the hell are you doing?!" I did learn an important lesson: however beautiful it may look from the outside, no one can know what something *really* is like and whether it's *really* right for you until you experience it for yourself. Things often look deceptively nice from the outside.

After completely immersing myself in modeling, I started noticing something else that had pretty much escaped my attention until then: the modeling world is full of drugs, sex, seedy people and powerful men.

I would look at my calendar and see I had a casting session that afternoon. Another one. Where? On an industrial estate, of course. Some remote location. My stomach dropped. But yes, of course I went, and upon arrival there'd always be a man there waiting for me. "Please go and get changed. I will see you back here in lingerie." Mega-creepy, mega-unsafe. The problem was that no one really realized it. It's hard to see when you're right in the middle of it. Not because it was actually normal, but because everyone seemed to consider it normal. In fact, I started to believe I was the abnormal one because of my attitude. It was considered normal to be left alone with men, even though I didn't know them and didn't feel comfortable with it. It was normal that they always asked if you could take off yet another piece of clothing, even though I really didn't want to. It was normal that they touched you without asking for permission, even though I would normally have never allowed anyone to do that. It was normal that all the other people on the set saw it happen, but didn't say anything. Because that's what happened day in, day out. It was also normal that many girls felt they couldn't turn down these work opportunities, nor say no to whatever these men asked them to do. After all, they had the power to break or make you. In my case it luckily never went too far, because ultimately I did find the courage to start setting boundaries. But I only did so after my limits had been pushed many times and I was way out of my comfort zone. It was just too normalized and too subtle to be able to pinpoint exactly what healthy boundaries were.

I think I can sum it up best by saying that as a young woman, I often felt unsafe. I'm sure many women will know what I'm talking about. Basically, just ask any woman what it feels like to walk on a deserted street at dusk. Women are also systematically taken advantage of. Unfortunately, I experienced firsthand that the modeling world is no different in that respect. From the outside, people mainly see the glitz and glamour, but on the inside it can be dirty and at times pitch-black.

Only after the whole storm of the #MeToo movement did I realize, "Hey, wait a minute... that's it! So it wasn't just me." I'm really glad we no longer accept something that is abnormal as normal. Although we still have a very long way to go. I prefer not to think back to that period of my life, since it usually makes me feel awful. It did teach me some personal lessons, however, things I will never forget. But still, I'd rather move on and leave it behind me. It has also taught me not to give someone else the key to my happiness. And yes, I could of course stand up and say those things were done to me, but what good would that do? When people tell me they see me as a strong woman, I think part of the reason is that strength isn't derived from everything that's in our favor. No, we become strong from the things that do not automatically go our way: when we're able to turn our vulnerability into strength. Every strong person has their own story that explains how and why they didn't have any other choice than to be strong.

"

Sometimes you
have to CHANGE
in order to
be *yourself.*

"

But what was I looking for in that world, you might wonder. And why did I choose to stay in it for a relatively long time? Good questions. In my early twenties, seeing the bigger picture wasn't one of my strong points yet. I was only able to do that after I stepped out of the modeling world. Only then did I notice the perfectionism, the high ambitions, the need to prove myself. I felt grateful for having been given this chance and wanted to do my very best. And I wanted to succeed, because people kept on saying: "You could definitely be a full-time model, Kelly." All right, I thought, but then I really want to go all the way. Why? Not because it was easy, that's for sure. I noticed the envious looks, and not only from a distance. "She thinks she's sooo pretty. She's a bit full of herself, isn't she?" The comments hit home, even though deep down inside I was still the same old busy bee, desperately seeking the approval of others. I resolved to give it my all, so that I wouldn't have any regrets. At the same time I also made a solemn promise to myself – something which would later prove to be a lifesaver: "I'll do this full-time for a year. If I don't like it then, I'll go back to university and finish my master's degree." That made it all very clear and narrowed down. I'd made my decision and was going to put in serious effort, but if I later discovered that it didn't suit me, I'd go back to school. All right, time to put my back into it, time for some can-do power! Because that's my standard approach: either all in or all out. If I'm going to do something, I might as well go the whole hog.

And yes, I was 21 years old, but mentally I felt more like 42. That's really what I thought. People said it all the time. "Kelly is so mature! That girl is an old soul." Yeah, right... I know better now. I wasn't 42, I was 21. Still a girl. It's not like I really was an adult, I just behaved like one. I also believed what people said about me, like: "Oh, she'll be fine, she'll manage." Asking for help was not an option; I am only now learning to do that. Just as I now know that I should listen to my gut feeling and allow my own happiness to be important. And that I can and should ask for help if I need it.

I thought I had pretty much left that period behind me, until one night in December 2015. I was watching a Dutch TV show, and the presenter, Peter van der Vorst, was visiting Dutch supermodel Romee Strijd in New York. When he asked her: "I can imagine it can get very lonely. Do you miss your friends?" she broke down. And I broke down with her. I cried and cried and cried. Everything suddenly came pouring out. The loneliness I had felt back then, the despair of what I had gotten myself into. What had I forced myself to do? What dangers had I exposed myself to? If I think back to all that now, the places I had to go to… The dark alleyways with doors that led to casting calls; all those locations where I was alone with photographers I didn't know. I don't even dare to imagine my own daughter doing something like that when she's older. And that's when it sunk in that I had downplayed it all the entire time – my standard response. Yes, of course there are always other people who might have been in a tighter spot or have faced more difficulties. But that doesn't mean that what happened to you is insignificant. Everyone has their own shit to deal with and is entitled to their own opinion and emotions. What I try to do is move forward, charge right through it and tackle things head-on, but at some point I also want to walk to the back door and leave it all behind me. There's no sense in dwelling on these kinds of things; it's not like I can change the past.

*

As a young woman I was calm, conscientious and very focused on what other people thought of me, but not necessarily insecure. My parents had done a great job in building up my self-esteem. Unfortunately it hit rock-bottom due to my stint in the modeling world, but those experiences also taught me a lot. For one thing, that period showed me that getting self-esteem from other people is impossible. That SELF in self-esteem is there for a reason, right? What do *I* think of myself? That's what counts, not what others think of me. That is not to say that we can only be self-confident when we love absolutely everything about ourselves, when we've achieved some sort of perfection. No, that's bullshit. I mean sure, if you're incredibly fond of your own stretch marks and rolls of fat – good for you. I just happen to be a woman who is not exactly crazy about cellulite. Just like I would also have preferred to have small, dainty feet instead of those size 10 gunboats of mine. I have, however, learned to give zero fucks about that. I don't focus on that kind of stuff anymore. And the same applies to my looks, my inner self, my milestones and actually pretty much everything that I think others might have more of, or be better at than me. I no longer care about that. Instead, I choose to focus on the things I *do* have and *am* happy with. Things do not have to be perfect to bring you joy. The only thing I need to know is how to stay joyful despite the ups and downs and the pros and cons.

In general, people are much better at seeing what others have going for them. When it comes to ourselves, we unfortunately mostly focus on what we lack. "Oh wow, just look at that gorgeous body of hers! Oh wow, he has such a great career! Oh wow, they have such a beautiful house! Oh wow, they really have the perfect relationship, don't they!" You're looking at others through rose-colored glasses, but seeing yourself through gray-tinted shades. And that makes all the difference! Who knows, she might have all sorts of health issues with that beautiful body of hers. Who knows, he might have a bad marriage despite or even *because of* that great career of his. What do appearances actually say about the reality behind them?

I wish everyone the very best and have chosen to focus on myself and on the positive as much as possible. And no, it's not like I get up in the morning, look in the mirror and shout: "Gee whiz, Kel, you're so amazingly kind, smart, funny and gorgeous!" (But if that works for you, please go ahead!) I have simply unlearned the habit of saying nasty or negative things to myself. I've unlearned the habit of focusing on what is lacking. I've simply accepted certain things about myself and am now choosing to focus on something else. And *that* has made me into a self-confident person. Stop comparing; stop disliking others or yourself; accept things as they are and focus on the things that really matter! Honestly, all the rest is a waste of time.

Questions you shouldn't ask yourself: "What does he or she think of me? Am I nice and likeable enough? Smart enough? Why does or doesn't she have this or that?" Stop comparing! But do ask yourself: "What do I think of myself? Do I like myself? Am I basically happy with myself? Am I happy with my life?" Someone else doesn't need to find you nice, attractive and smart, nor do they have to understand your choices. You choose; it's your life. See what happens as soon as you change how you talk to yourself? I chose to focus on the wrong things for far too long – on what I wasn't able to do, on things I wasn't good at, on what I didn't succeed in, and on all the things I didn't like about myself and what everyone who disliked me said about me. Letting thoughts like that dominate our mindset not only makes us insecure, but eventually makes us utterly miserable. Choose to focus on the things that lift you up. Walk your own path, and if you find it doesn't bring you joy, dare to change direction and take a different route.

I'm extra careful about which internal and external voices I listen to. I make sure I say positive, constructive things to myself. I do the same online, meaning I don't follow people that make me insecure and I don't look at social media accounts or news platforms that only spark negativity. In my inner circle, I no longer make room for people who are not supportive. (More on that later in the chapter about friendship.) And I no longer let anyone else determine whether I am worthy or not. The secret to self-esteem is not that you shouldn't care about what other people think of you, it's making your own opinion about yourself way more important. Of course I listen to feedback from people that I care about, but even then I'm still the only one who gets to determine what I think of myself. I've realized how important your mindset is for your degree of self-esteem. Here too, I can make my own choices, and I want to choose the things that make me happier. In my thoughts and in my actions.

*

I was back in Milan for a business trip a while ago. I found myself walking down a street I instantly recognized. It was etched in my memory, even though I was still a young woman the last time I was there. It was the street where I went to the all-important casting call that triggered the power of choice in me. It was for a show by one of the world's biggest fashion houses and they handed me an outfit that I didn't fit into; there was just no way I could get the pants buttoned. With a deep sigh, they eventually found me something else to wear. Dressed in that new outfit, I introduced myself to the casting director. She looked me over from head to foot and barked: "What size do you wear?!" Before I could so much as reply "I'm a 6," she looked visibly annoyed and shouted: "Thank you, NEXT!!!"

I walked out of there thinking that would be the very last "next" I ever heard as a model. I was so incredibly fed up with only feeling worthwhile as long as I conformed to someone else's ideals of beauty. I booked a ticket back to the Netherlands – a one-way ticket this time – intending to put a lot of work into my studies, promising myself I would definitely travel the world again, but this time on my own terms.

Standing there in that street in Milan again, but now as an entrepreneur, was a pivotal "I've come full circle" sort of moment. I was glad that bitch had sent me away that day, thus giving me the final push to no longer let my self-esteem be determined by others. It is a real treat to know that I am now earning my own living by following my passion – and can choose my own pants size, too!

"

Life already has
enough CHALLENGES.
You *don't* have to be
one yourself.

"

LOVE

In 2012, I went back to Utrecht University to get my master's degree in Clinical and Health Psychology, just like I had intended. After my travels around the world, I did have to adjust to the normal structure of life and somehow find my feet. A long-term relationship ended and I decided I wanted to stay single for a while, to figure out exactly what I wanted, in love and in life. And as these things go, love finds you when you're not looking for it. Love at first sight – been there – but this was different. This was fun at first sight. And totally fascinating. We cracked each other up and were evenly matched. But the whole thing did make me say to myself, "No way, Kel, don't go there..."

I remember it as if it were yesterday, suddenly seeing John's face on Facebook. The only thing that jumped to mind was: "Ooooh, what a hottie!" Of course I also recognized him from the TV program *Idols.* He'd been one of the judges, and I had already been swooning over his looks then. Well, I have to admit I'm old for my years and have always had a soft spot for slightly older men. We turned out to have a ton of Facebook friends in common and I kept repeating to myself: "Kel, you do remember what you agreed with yourself, right? Don't take life so seriously. Come on, just friend him on Facebook!" It didn't take long for him to ask me out to dinner. I can still hear my sister saying: "Hellooooo, you're single! One date isn't going to hurt, is it?!" My mother chipped in: "Look, of course it's never going to turn into anything serious, but it's not like you have to marry the guy." Well uh... we're now ten years and two kids later.

If I had stuck to my list of what my Mr. Right had to have, I would never have met John. In retrospect, it's pretty hilarious that people make these kinds of lists to begin with, defining the (usually very superficial) personality traits that someone has to have to be a perfect match, since nothing could be further from the truth. But yeah, I also had a list in mind while looking for a partner. And I even found the 'perfect match', a guy who ticked all the boxes. He was good-looking, had the right degree and a nice family, and was a hard-working achiever. But it turned out we lacked the traits to bring out the best in each other.

It was a great example of how I had used logic to figure out what kind of guy would be a good partner. And yes, of course I also took into account whether my family and friends would approve of him. So what did I learn from all this? That when it comes to love, we definitely shouldn't let our brain do all the thinking. Sure, keeping your wits about you is smart if you're looking for long-lasting love, but my advice is to start off by listening to your heart. In the end my perfect match turned out to be someone who couldn't have been more different from my rational idea of a good match. So no, love has nothing to do with wanting to be picture perfect, but is about sensing what kind of person would be right for you. And even though it might feel good and seem right, that doesn't automatically mean things will magically take care of themselves.

*

In matters of the heart, we usually automatically think of the other person and tend to forget that our relationship with ourselves is actually more important. So I'd rather not talk about love here while skipping over the most important part: self-love. I have to admit that the word "self-love" always gets on my nerves. It sounds a bit too new-age flaky, and I've reframed it in very practical terms. Because it's very simple, really. If you don't love yourself, it becomes very difficult for someone else to love you. As I already mentioned in the chapter about self-esteem, loving yourself doesn't imply that you get up, look in the mirror and shout out how awesome you are. Loving yourself comes down to making choices that make you a happier person. Practicing self-care in terms of healthy nutrition and enough exercise. Taking a break or asking for help when needed. Being less hard on yourself. Being kind to yourself! Gathering supportive people around you who wish you well. Setting boundaries and sticking to them.

Self-love is also about embracing imperfections, however. Accepting what is. Daring to be yourself. Daring to walk your own path. Answering the question "what do I really want?" and having the courage to go for that. Self-love is giving yourself the love and appreciation we hope to receive from others, from our children, a partner or a friend. But it all starts with loving yourself. Please know that you really can give yourself that love.

66

The most *important*
RELATIONSHIP
you will ever have
is THE ONE
with *yourself.*

99

I discovered that I used to put up with certain behavior from other people – in romantic relationships as well – because I hadn't yet figured out what I wanted and needed. It wasn't distressing or anything, but I was a people-pleaser and liked to be appreciated. That meant I ended up letting others cross boundaries, either because I didn't yet know where my boundaries were, or because I struggled to define them clearly. In that respect, love has really helped me realize how wonderful making mistakes can be. Boyfriends, crushes and flings – even the wrong ones – helped me determine what I did and didn't want. And then I also started seeing my own role in the whole thing very clearly. Instead of thinking, "Oh no, poor me! What a coincidence that I'm meeting yet another douchebag," try this for a change: "What is it about me that always seems to attract jerks? How can I love myself more and attract supportive people instead? And if I notice that they don't have my best interests at heart, how can I be self-confident enough to show them the door right away?"

I also had to acknowledge that I had my own hang-ups about romantic relationships. Learn to own those, instead of making somebody else responsible for them. I had plenty of shit from the past that complicated my relationships. In both romantic relationships and friendships, for instance, I have had to deal with jealousy as well as lying and infidelity. Of course I could have just stayed there on the couch, moping jealously, and told my partner he was not allowed to go out. But wouldn't it be smarter to do something about my own insecurity? To figure out what the root causes are and how to overcome those? There are certain issues only I can tackle; no one else can do that for me. Want to keep things fun? Then don't make someone else responsible for solving your issues. Sure, it's great if a partner helps you, but that other person is not the solution. In any case, I decided to work on that myself.

From previous relationships, I gradually learned what I ultimately wanted from a loving connection. For example, I often fell for people who were my polar opposite. But in my experience opposites usually clash, certainly in the long term. In the beginning, a totally dissimilar boyfriend would mean excitement, passion, sparks. But then, within no time, he would start seriously getting under my skin. It taught me that I basically want someone to be on more or less the same page. I'm a homebody, so I don't want to be in a relationship with someone who has ants in their pants. Nor with someone who likes a quiet, steady life, while I enjoy the occasional splurge. Nor with someone who has no ambition at all, while I'm extremely driven. Nor with someone who's not the least bit dominant, while

I can be a bit of a bulldozer. Nor with someone who has totally different values. And why not? Quite simply because I just don't feel like arguing about all that. When two people are *that* different, it causes friction. And I know what that's like – so no, I'm not looking for that in a partner. In the end, "what am I really looking for?" is the eternal question that keeps popping back up. That's why it's so important to get to know yourself, because then you'll be able to identify what you want in life and in love.

Too often I hear people say: "I'm looking for someone who will make me happy." Or: "If only he would make me happier." Yeah right, sounds wonderful, but it doesn't really work like that, does it? The other person can't make you happy. Make yourself happy first, and be sure to figure out exactly what makes you happy. Please don't get me wrong: asking yourself "How happy does someone make me?" is a good question. But it should be a follow-up, not the starting point. The very first questions are: "How happy do I make myself? And do I actually have a clue how to make myself happy?" Self-love is knowing your own true value and giving yourself what you deserve. And you certainly don't need anyone else to do that for you. As a result, you start attracting people who see your true value and give you what you deserve.

However, self-love also has to do with not putting up with your own crap. And like I said, it's important that we don't make other people responsible for things we have to solve ourselves. Don't make someone else responsible for your own toxic behavior. Don't let someone who really likes you have to pay for what someone else did to you in the past. Identify your own personal development challenges and acknowledge that your partner is not the source. In short, make sure to solve your own relationship issues first, so that you can come together as a couple and both focus on the other obstacles you have to overcome together.

*

A garden where the flowers are watered, the plants are pruned and the garden beds are occasionally weeded looks much better than one that isn't maintained. This applies to just about everything in life. Everything works as long as we put in the work. Investing time and energy is a conscious choice. I'm very mindful about which priorities I want to focus on at different times of my life – more about that later in the chapter about ambition – and love is one of those. I consciously choose to devote my energy to love. Not that I necessarily always feel like doing that, but it's important for my happiness. For me, falling in love is something that happens pretty naturally, and because of the infatuation in the beginning, everything else follows pretty naturally too. But inevitably, after a while we all tumble from cloud nine and lose the rose-colored glasses. In the beginning it's still kind of charming that he leaves all his stuff lying around – he's such an adorably disorganized slob – but a year later, you'd rather chuck it all out: "Hey, do you think I am your slave or something?!"

I really like how Tony Robbins puts it. If you treat people at the end of the relationship like you did in the beginning, there won't be an end. People gladly do everything for their significant other when they've just met. "Oh yeah, sure, I'll tidy up for you. Oh, don't worry, I'll pop by the grocery store and also get you some flowers. No, of course I don't mind doing that!" In that scenario, we focus on the problem, assign it a positive label and commit ourselves to finding a solution. However, when we assign a negative label the issue of the 'empty refrigerator' – "Dammit, now I have to go to the store for you *again*!" – that's not going to improve the relationship. Don't get me wrong, a conversation about a fair division of household chores is certainly appropriate; I was just illustrating what a difference it can make in how much time and energy you're willing to spend on each other.

Communication is key in all of this. I happen to be a bit of an emotional flatliner. I'm unflappable and overall quite balanced in life. In a relationship, I communicate clearly; I say it like it is. If something bothers me, I speak my mind, but without splitting hairs. In my view, the trick is to avoid making mountains out of molehills. Pick your battles, that's my motto. Save the serious discussions for the things that really matter, because making a fuss about everything could drive you both insane. By expressing what bothers me, I get it off my chest and avoid a bad mood by bottling up issues that are important to me. Better to have it out in the open.

Gary Chapman's book *The Five Languages of Love* was quite an eyeopener in that respect. He aptly describes how the world is full of languages: from English to Mandarin, from Swahili to Catalan. Most people don't have a clue what someone who speaks a foreign language is trying to convey. The same goes for love. Do you actually speak the same love language as your partner? I found out that my language of love is 'acts of service'. Partly because of those tough years of hard work, I consider helpfulness an act of love, like when someone does something for me, organizes something or just takes some weight off my shoulders. Basically, just offers me a helping hand. When I tried to figure out where that habit of mine came from, I realized it wasn't just that demanding period in my life, but also because I find it difficult to ask for help, since I'm always telling myself that I'm a strong, independent woman. So kudos to the person who helps me out without me having to ask for help!

It had seriously never occurred to me that John might speak a completely different love language. That's why I started doing a lot of things for him, although his language was much more about positive words and compliments. Guess what? As soon as you start communicating your needs better, someone else can fulfil them more effectively. Then there's no risk of constantly bringing home flowers when your partner actually gets a fluttery feeling from seeing you emptying the dishwasher. And it also won't be necessary to go to great pains to arrange a romantic dinner, knowing that your partner responds well to compliments and the occasional "I love you". By having a better understanding of your own behavior and your partner's, you can anticipate each other's needs better. A close connection is only possible by being aware of what both partners want and need. Because at the end of the day, we all want to feel important to someone, especially when it comes to love.

*

All my major life-changing experiences piled up and came together over the past ten years. Moving in together, having my career take off, starting my own businesses, my own life, having children, getting engaged, changing friendships, facing health challenges and loss. We experienced all these big life events together. The transition from being a woman to a mother was huge. How that changes your life in general – and your relationship – is quite simply colossal. It's as if the entire development process takes place in a pressure cooker. I was essentially still the same person, but my entire life was turned upside down. And I really needed time to recover from that. It's so important to stay connected to your own feelings and express what your needs are, since those change with every new stage in life. And when you're already struggling with that yourself – and sometimes even lose yourself a bit along the way – you shouldn't expect your partner to be capable of flawlessly guessing what's going on and always staying connected to the real you. Try to grow together and take each other by the hand. And accept that friction is part of it.

What's my number-one relationship insight? Truly making time for each other, truly making time for love. Especially during those hectic years, it's smart to keep a close eye on the balance and cadence in your schedule. In that period of your life, spending time together is almost never a given, so don't take it for granted. Seize those moments! Ensure there's time for difficult conversations and for nice, relaxing chats. Make time to laugh together, to act a bit crazy now and then, to do exciting stuff and to just basically really *be* with each other. And yes, the same applies to sex. I like to put it this way: if the sex is good, it accounts for 10 percent of your relationship; if it's bad, it takes up 90 percent. It's important to consciously choose and to invest time and energy in your sex life. Keep communicating about your needs. And yeah, okay, I have to admit I'm also a very practical person, so I just schedule it in. Want to wait for that one spontaneous romantic moment? Then please know that there will be periods of your life when that means you might be in for a loooooong wait. In my opinion, a solid basis for a good relationship is wanting to do things for each other, to listen to each other, to want to spend time together and to have an open mind and be willing to understand each other.

*

The problematic thing about love is that most people tend to be unrealistic. We set the bar so unbelievably high. We want it all, and we want it all at once: relationship, career, children, social life, physical exercise, excitement, but also R&R and time for ourselves, as well as time for each other. But hey, a relationship is not just a long series of highlights and peak moments. It's also about accepting that not everything is possible and to be satisfied, even if you do not have it all at the same time. And about being okay with that. However, that can be a challenge, because someone other than your partner could suddenly become extremely interesting. There's a reason that cheating is so common. After all, with that secret crush you don't have to argue about all kinds of day-to-day things, like the toilet seat being left up, the missing cap on the toothpaste or all the hair in the shower drain.

We can condemn infidelity or examine the root cause. Fact is: if you want to stay together for a long time, it's important to accept that it means going through different life stages together. Sometimes people lose touch with themselves a little bit and need to recalibrate their own needs first. During this whole process, it's unrealistic to assume that you won't run the risk of losing each other a little bit as well. And that's okay, as long as you find each other again. Sometimes it works out fine, sometimes less so, but that's just the reality of spending your life together. People either grow with each other or they grow apart; it's as simple as that.

Love is, however, by far the most important area in life where the choice should first and foremost be about what makes you happy. Does the other person make you unhappy? Then leave! At least, that's what I did. And I also did something else: I broke up with someone even though our relationship wasn't bad or anything. Things were fine, everything was okay, but I wanted more. Please remember that everyone is entitled to not having to settle for less than true happiness. But the trick is to actually be content once you're happy. My current relationship is not a dream relationship, John is not Mr. Right, nor am I Miss Perfect. We have a real relationship and feel real love for each other. And yes, sometimes that requires hard work.

If there's one thing love has taught me, it's to no longer be bothered by lists, nor by perfection and certainly not by the opinions of others. I am choosing to feel the love there is, am prepared to work for it, to do things in the way I and my partner want to do them, using my own happiness as a guideline, regardless of what other people might think. In love, we shouldn't settle for less than what we're worth, nor for less than our own happiness. At the same time, love also means being realistic and content. Nobody is perfect. Not you, nor your partner.

These are some of the questions I no longer ask myself when it comes to love: "What do others think of my partner? What do others think of my relationship? Why do other people seem to have absolutely great relationships?" Much smarter questions to bear in mind are: "How do I make myself happy? How can someone else make me even happier? How can we be happy together? And how can I keep things really good despite the inevitable ups and downs?"

In the end, others have nothing to do with how you choose to live your life, let alone your love life. Don't be concerned with their opinion, let it go! How people want to organize their life is their business. Why should I even have an opinion about that? Many people have all sorts of ideas about relationships and how other people manage their love life. Don't worry about that, because hey, it's not like they need to be in a relationship with you or your partner, right?!

*

I inherited my no-nonsense attitude from my parents and grandparents, and that has helped me a lot in matters of love. They taught me there's a reason someone is your partner; you don't just pack your bags when the going gets tough. I also had the chance to see that they had mastered the art of going through life without ridiculously high expectations. They knew all too well that life is not all roses or a long series of highlights. The same applies to love. Problems? Worries? Misery and death? Yup, it's all part of the deal. How do we cope with that? Face it. Solve it. Don't paint an overly rosy picture of life. Problems are there to be confronted, not to be avoided. Charge right through and tackle them head-on! When I have a discussion with someone, I see it as a means to solve something. It's a way to be able to keep looking each other straight in the eye. Don't run the risk of harboring grudges, but just BAM! put all the cards on the table. And no, that's not always fun, but it is necessary to keep things fun.

Both online and in our immediate environment, things can appear to be simple and easy, but love requires a lot of work. Getting together isn't difficult, but staying together is. Real love doesn't just happen by itself. Of course there should be moments when it does flow naturally and when it feels wonderful the entire time, but love is also about constant communication, learning lessons and achieving acceptance. For me, love has always had its ups and downs; the trick is to find love that is 100 percent worth fighting for. When you find yourself surreptitiously gazing at the oh-so-green grass of the other side of the fence, remind yourself that it's probably artificial turf. And if it isn't, the neighbors sure use a lot of shit as fertilizer! Perfect relationships and Mr. Rights and Miss Perfects simply don't exist. Don't let the chance of love pass you by because you believe in a fantasy straight out of a romance novel. Perfect doesn't exist anywhere. The perfect place to start is self-love, because how can we ever love someone else if we can't even give ourselves that love? Stop comparing, quit constantly worrying and having doubts. Focus on yourself and on your relationship: with yourself or with someone else. What would *you* like? What do you want from life? From love? And what do you want to give someone else? Not all relationships last, and that's okay. Whatever happens, it teaches us lessons and helps us grow. By opening your heart and being willing to put in the work – on your own, but together as well – it will all turn out fine in the end. The most beautiful things often appear in a less immediate and less easily recognizable form. Keep an open mind, get out there, kiss the occasional frog and just see what happens! A partner doesn't have to be perfect to be perfect for you.

"

Love does
not have to
be PERFECT
to be perfect
for YOU.

"

FRIENDSHIP

My days were filled with studying, internships and a new boyfriend. Only now I started noticing that there was a lot of friction between me and some of my friends. They'd been enjoying student life together all those years, while I'd been extremely serious about my work. Modeling jobs were always very last-minute offers, and sometimes I would have to go abroad at short notice, so I really was AWOL more often than not. I attended very few parties and dinners. I did feel bad about that, but I'd made the choice to go all-out for work. I had the discipline to put 'fun' on the back burner, and wanted to do well for myself. And besides, although I had always liked going out, it was never all that often, and certainly not pulling all-nighters with loads of booze. I'm just not super social; I'm more of a quality-time person. So then the others were like: "Oh, don't bother inviting her, she never has time anyway," while I was like: "Yeah, but wait, guys! I'll join in again soon!"

Little by little, I was sidelined. I'd find out they had gotten together without inviting me. And I started hearing that I was being talked about behind my back. "Oh yeah, she's Miss Netherlands now, and she kicked her boyfriend out and doesn't care about anything else anymore." I totally understood that not everyone got how I lived my life and the choices that came with it, because they would have had to experience it themselves to know what it was like. That's the only way they would have understood you don't simply decline a modeling job because of a party. And besides, I'd worked so hard to get where I was. Partying all night and stuffing yourself with junk food is exactly what you want to avoid when you're going to great pains to stay in shape for a bikini shoot. It might be boring, but discipline and perseverance are crucial to succeed.

My relationship was also growing increasingly serious; we were really enjoying life and love together. And although some of my friends were equally delighted with my achievements and encouraged me whenever I faced a challenge, I noticed that others didn't understand it at all, and some were jealous. The knot in my stomach grew and grew because I felt left out and because people thought I had changed. They didn't include me in their conversations and plans anymore. And my reaction to all this? I tried harder and harder to be liked...

Since I'd just left a period full of insecurity behind me, I had to find my confidence again. The voice of that bitch from Milan might have been silenced, but I did listen to the voices of other people around me, people who maybe no longer had my best interests at heart. I listened to their opinions and to the little voice in my head that kept telling me I was a lousy friend. Since I was extremely loyal, choosing to fight for these friendships seemed the logical choice. It got worse, but I kept trying to hold on to something that didn't suit me anymore. Why? Because I was asking myself the wrong questions. Questions that didn't help me choose my own happiness.

I was great at worrying though. "How can I be a better friend? How can I make them like me more? How can I prove that I'm still the same old Kelly? How can I ensure I'm part of the group again?" And you know, looking back, I think this might be typical for women. Many men seem to be fine when they don't talk and hardly see each other for years or when their lives take a totally different course. And then as soon as they meet up again over some beers, they just pick off where they left off. Women really seem to be wired differently.

For a long time, I thought, "Oh no, it's my fault! I have to change; I should make even more of an effort." I'd bend over backwards to be able to join in. I increasingly became the sort of person I thought others wanted me to be. Fearing envy, I was increasingly vague about what was going on in my life. Fearing people would talk about me in my absence. Fearing I was different. And at no point did I ask myself the right questions: "Wait a minute, what do I want? What do I expect from a friendship? Do I still want to be part of this? What's in it for me?"

By that time, my work ethic had afforded me a nice financial buffer. I was planning to use most of my savings to set up my own practice after getting my master's degree. But I'd also leased a Fiat 500. I vividly remember the evening I drove to a dinner party a friend had organized. Oh man, I was so incredibly proud! I turned into my friend's street and decided to park a few blocks further down, to avoid any nasty remarks. To my ears, the more and more frequent half-joking comment of "Jeez, you are always soooo lucky!" sounded as if they didn't think I deserved it. I hated it and was disappointed in myself that I didn't just park in front of her house, because in her case, I would have rushed outside and drooled along with my bestie over her new car or bike or private jet – whatever.

When I played back all the conversations in my head later, I was shocked. Yes, people had inquired about my life, that wasn't the problem. They asked questions ranging from "So how are you? How is your love life?" to "And how's work?" But it was my own answers that made no sense at all. I just blathered on and on, beating about the bush since it no longer felt safe to share things. Inside me, my intuition was screaming, "Shut up!" I didn't dare tell anyone how serious my romantic relationship had become. About all the fun things we were doing. I didn't say anything about how well my internship was going. How my very first client had been so happy with her therapy she'd bought me flowers, and that I had welled up with tears when she gave them to me.

Driving home after the dinner party, I had a sinking feeling in my stomach. I had to face the truth: with a part of my inner circle, I just couldn't be myself anymore. Later, at home, on the couch, bawling my eyes out, it finally sunk in: it was over. This had been going on for so long now, and it had to stop. If I couldn't be myself anymore, then friendship was impossible. I knew I had to say goodbye. I wasn't sure how yet, but I did know this wasn't what I wanted.

*

I had to learn that some friendships last a lifetime, but others are merely transient. Saying goodbye isn't fun and sometimes so downright shitty that it feels like going through all stages of grief. Eventually, it's a huge relief though. Sometimes it's better to part ways, to create some space for yourself again – as well as space for new people, people who are a better match. For me, this was a whole process. I would constantly second-guess myself. Had I really changed that much? Frankly: no. I'd always been me; I'd just stopped always saying "fine" and "sure" and "nice". I increasingly dared to take a stand about the things I liked and found important in life. I guess that's actually quite normal when you get older. I've always been pretty serious and focused, and my main focus was on my career, finding a nice partner, settling down and starting a family. A couple of friends knew all this and would react with remarks like: "Oh, I'm so happy for you!" The rest said: "So what are you up to these days?" when I occasionally would decline opportunities to go out, because I also wanted to devote time to my studies. And after a while that became: "Yeah, we didn't bother inviting you, 'cause you never have time anyway."

I honestly don't think I changed; I actually started finding myself. Some friendships were not strong enough to survive that. It was partly my own fault, because I guess there was a time when I didn't know well enough what I wanted, so I couldn't express well enough what I needed and struggled with. But there is another side to it as well: people around you need to allow you to be yourself. They need to support you in how you want to lead your life, because those choices bring you joy, even though your friends might make completely different choices themselves. And maybe you also handled things differently before, but you've grown since then. Especially when you've been friends for a long time and you were both very young when you met, it's obvious that you will both change and possibly develop in different ways. It's important to allow each other that personal growth. For me, it's super important that the people in my inner circle are happy. And the most beautiful insight is that I now also have the courage to allow myself to expect that in return.

"

The *only* people
who have a problem
with you setting
BOUNDARIES are
the ones who
take advantage of you
not having them.

"

For far too long, I asked myself the wrong questions. Yes, it's good to think about how you can be a better friend. But it's smarter to first consider these questions: "What do I look for in a friendship? What values should a good friendship be based on, in my opinion?" And only go all-out for someone after that has been taken care of. Had I realized this sooner, I would have decided to call it quits much earlier. I was out of my comfort zone for far too long, wanting to keep the peace. And when being yourself – albeit a more developed version – means you can't have a future together, then it's not meant to be. In that case you're doing each other a favor by parting ways, because continuing would only cause frustration. Beautiful friendships are an important ingredient for my happiness. Please make time and create space for yourself to allow the right people to be part of your life.

*

I believe the same applies to family. People often think that because you're related, family automatically always has to see eye to eye. That because it's family, they are allowed unlimited access to our time and energy. I've been lucky to have a very close-knit family. Not that the relationship has always been perfect, but we've always been close. We're four generations and essentially, we're all on the same page. This is why they still hold a prime spot in my inner circle, because they believe in the same core values that I look for in friendships. We certainly don't always agree on things, and we may lead different lives, but we give each other freedom in that. Had that been different, I would have done something about it, just like I do with regular friendships these days. Cutting contact with a family member – especially when it's someone close to you in terms of loyalty, like a parent or sibling – is of course incredibly difficult and not a decision to be taken lightly, but sometimes there is no other way. I have plenty of friends who unfortunately are old hands at that game, and it's never easy, but sometimes it really was the only solution. I've seen it so often, watching people suffer because of their firm conviction that after all, family is family and blood is thicker than water, only to see them flourish as soon as they set clear boundaries. And those are necessary in all relationships, whether with a lover, a friend or a relative. Please remember that the only people who will have a problem with the fact that you set boundaries are the ones who benefit from you not having them.

People often do things or accept certain situations *because* it's family. Try turning it around! The question we should be asking ourselves is whether we'd still find it acceptable if it *wasn't* family. The fact that it *is* family doesn't mean we should accept behavior that we wouldn't put up with from others. Even though we're someone's grandchild, cousin, child or sibling, we're all adults with lives of our own. And you're allowed to decide for yourself how you want to live your life. A family member's opinions, as well as their beliefs and habits, are exactly that: theirs, not yours. You're allowed to lead your life exactly as you please. And you also have the right to handle things the way you want to handle them. Don't get me wrong, it's always good to keep an open mind and listen to other people's views. And it's great if other people approve of the way you handle things. But if that's not the case, that's okay too! Just put them on mute or give people less of your time.

And yes, your family will always be your family; you get them for free, no extra charge. Which means you can't always choose which people will play a role in your life. What you can determine, however, is if you want to give them your time – and if so, how much. The power of choice! And you know what? How long a friendship or a family tie lasts says virtually nothing about how good that relationship is for you. What does count is whether you feel free to be yourself when you're with them.

Whether it's friendships or family ties, daring to zoom out and looking at the bigger picture is important. Which people are part of your inner circle and how do you want to invest or divide your time? Who is allowed to criticize you? Because criticism is not something to be avoided – it can be super useful. But please do ask yourself: "Who says what, and is that person important to me? Is it someone who wishes me well? Is it worthwhile for me to listen to their opinion and take it to heart? Do I want to keep an open mind to what they have to say?" Those are all important questions. Because you never know you might otherwise have to listen to your mother-in-law's interminable advice on how to raise children, while you're actually living in the same house as her own child and seeing first-hand every single day that she didn't exactly dot all the i's and cross all the t's in her own parenting. You don't want to do that. Advice is great, but be mindful of which voices you listen to and when you just want to walk your own path. And remember that it's your choice to determine which voices you want to put on mute and which people you do want to give your time to.

*

Get to know yourself, so you will know what you want; that's a relevant truth for all areas of life. Not only will you be able to give yourself those things, but you can also communicate clearly how others can do that. Getting to know myself better paid off in friendships as well. And yes, unfortunately that lesson is often learned the hard way, precisely by ending up in difficult situations when things don't go smoothly – when you hurt each other or feel sad, angry or betrayed. As a kid, you become friends with someone because that other person happened to go to the same playground or be in the same class at school, but as you get older the core values of a friendship become more and more important. And the other person's core values need to be aligned with our own. It's become more than clear to me, for instance, that I don't like drama. People who make mountains out of molehills? No, thank you. The same goes for people who constantly want to claim my time; I need to have some space, without feeling like the other person is measuring the degree of closeness in our friendship by how many texts I send or how often I call them. I prefer to have friends around me that prioritize quality. When we're there, we're *really* there. And there's no question that we'll be there for each other in a crisis. But life can get really busy, and I'd like to be able to give each other enough breathing space to lead our life in a way that brings us joy. I'm actually a bit of a cactus; I'm very low-maintenance. Just the occasional downpour and a dash of plant food, and I'm good to go. I do best with friends who are like me in that respect. So don't make me team up with a difficult houseplant that needs constant TLC and is a challenge to maintain. A friendship like that ends up in the compost bin in no time.

In my opinion everyone should evaluate a friendship now and then. Ask yourself: "How do I actually build and maintain friendships? What do I want to devote my time to? Which people give me positive energy?" Why would you invest an incredible amount of time in an emotionally draining friendship, when it's basically just negativity and stress? If you notice those kinds of patterns, saying goodbye to those people will give you a sense of freedom, relief and breathing space. Look for people who bring out your best emotions. People you want to be with when you're feeling great, but also when you're feeling like shit. Regardless of whether you're related by blood. In order to have and keep the right people in my inner circle, I'm no longer going to ask myself: "How long have we been friends now? What have we been through together? What have I done for this person? Are we family?" And I'd like to advise you to ask yourself instead: "To what extent can I be myself with this person? Do we give each other enough space? Are we willing to understand each other?" Frankly, how long I've been friends with someone doesn't mean much to me. The same applies to family. For me, the most important criterion is the extent to which I can be myself. And there are different stages you go through in a friendship, naturally, just like in a romantic relationship. Sometimes life sends challenges your way, causing you both to understand each other a little less and lose sight of each other for a while. But a good friendship will survive. This holds true even when one of you temporarily has to make more of an effort, because it shouldn't be about who is doing 'more'; it's not a scale that has to balance out. Relationships go through different phases, but watch out when it becomes a structural issue and someone drains your energy. When it's giving you more negative than positive vibes. And when that's not a temporary thing.

*

Which people and what situations do you invite into your life? I like to put it this way: a good door policy works wonders. I chose to adopt an 'invite-only' policy years ago, and am very happy I did. How does it work? Think of your life as a party and realize that the best gift you can give yourself is only handing out invitations to people who actually make your life a party!

Some relationships come into your life to help you realize what no longer suits you. My inner circle is solid as a rock, which feels good. I flourish when I'm surrounded by friends who support me and vice versa. Who talk about me just as positively in my absence as when I'm there. Who would mention my name in a situation full of opportunities and put me forward, just like I would for them. Who I can celebrate good news with and who share theirs with me. Some of my friends I've known since elementary school, others I met as a student in the sorority I joined, some friends walked into my life around the same time as my partner, and some of them I only met a few years ago. Some are very similar to me, while others are completely different. And I love that, because the overriding principle is that we're unconditionally there for each other. We laugh together and cry together and everything in between. From the wildest nights to the toughest times, we experience it all together. We trust each other, can be honest with each other and respect each other for who we are.

"What is your number-one insight when it comes

to friendship?" people often ask me. "That it's better to have fewer people around you who matter more to you," is my standard reply. I guess for a long time I felt pressured to hold on to people because we came from the same childhood context or were already friends in elementary school. I put up with the fact that I couldn't be myself with them anymore and had the feeling I had to walk on eggshells. When we saw each other or talked on the phone, it usually left me drained instead of energized. Only once I realized how much my inner circle affected my happiness, did I dare to reduce or break off contact. Nowadays, I would never stay friends that long, let alone become friends – not when it's clear it won't work out for me. As I said before, how long you've been friends or whether you're related says virtually nothing about how good that relationship is for you. In the end, you can only know if it's working out when you feel free to be yourself with that person. The biggest lesson I learned is to keep listening to my feelings. How do I feel when I'm with someone? For me – now more than ever – it's about quality, not quantity.

66

This chapter
of MY LIFE is
invite-only!

99

MOTHERHOOD

I've always known I wanted to be a mother. Actually, that's the only thing I've ever seriously and very consciously wished for. My idea of true happiness has always been to have a nice home and my own family. And it might have been naïve of me, but I always felt that having kids was a choice. Either you want to have children, or you don't. And yes, I definitely wanted kids! So for me, the main two questions were: who will I have kids with, and when. The concept that I would one day become a mother was self-evident. And so I remember it as if it were yesterday, lying on the couch watching a Dutch TV show that follows couples during their adoption procedure. The young woman on the screen was explaining why she wanted to adopt a child. She was infertile due to the growth inhibitors she had taken as an adolescent, to prevent herself from becoming even taller than she already was. These pills apparently had side effects that were only discovered later, one of those being a high probability of infertility. She would have loved to have children of their own, but unfortunately it was no longer possible.

I shot upright; that casual statement hit me like a bombshell. Wait a minute, infertile due to growth inhibitors!? I had also taken those as a teenager! I started googling like mad and a long list of results popped up on my screen about reduced fertility as a result of hormone treatment. I've always been tall and gangly, towering over all my friends. That's still the case with my 5'11", but thanks to the inhibitors I decided to take, I never reached the predicted 6'3" – and boy, am I relieved that didn't happen. Apart from temporary weight gain, there were no known side effects at the time. As you can imagine, I was in complete shock at the news. I'd gone through life with the idea I'd be a mother some day and still had all the time in the world... And now it was maybe already too late?!

I immediately made an appointment with an OB/GYN. And after some tests, bingo, she discovered that my reproductive system did indeed show signs of aging. What did that mean? "Well, once you hit thirty, it's quite possible that your body will be that of a forty-year-old woman in terms of fertility. And early menopause has a huge impact on the likelihood of becoming pregnant. I see no reason why you shouldn't be able to get pregnant, but I'd advise you to keep in mind that it could take a while. If you don't manage to get pregnant within twelve months, come back and we'll see what we can do." I still remember walking across the parking lot to my car in a daze. Basically, she'd just told me that if I wanted to have children, I shouldn't wait any longer. Well, no way was I going to wait another minute after this doctor's appointment!

Months went by, and every month I'd sit there staring at another negative pregnancy test. Even before becoming a mother, motherhood was already my biggest lesson ever in learning how to let go. Obviously, stress has a negative impact on conception, but it's pretty darn impossible to *not* think about getting pregnant when you've both decided you want to go for it. But with this new info in the back of my mind, I couldn't seem to shake off the sneaky thought: "Surely not..." What does one do in that case? Which option would you choose? Anything you pay attention to grows, and when you focus on the negative, that grows too. I tried to stay positive and to avoid stress as much as possible. The things I wrote about in my first two books were also a huge help in staying calm. Like changing your mindset when you go through a rough patch, how to relieve stress and anxiety, how to change your focus.

Meanwhile, it had been almost a year since my OB/GYN appointment. I'd done a gazillion pregnancy tests and had deluded myself a gazillion times that I was indeed suffering from all kinds of pregnancy-related ailments. But over and over, I had to deal with the disappointment of yet another negative result. Until April 30th, Queen's Day, an annual national holiday in the Netherlands. We were planning to go out for drinks with friends and although I didn't have any clear physical symptoms, I decided to do a test just in case since I'd probably be drinking wine that afternoon. Minutes later, there I was, this time sitting down and staring flabbergasted at the display: *1-2 weeks pregnant.* For fuck's sake, I was actually pregnant! A dream come true! Sometimes you just have to be lucky in life, and I sure was…

*

At the time, I had no idea the birth of a child also means the birth of a mother, and that this change in role would feel like a raging storm. It turned out that my day-to-day reality differed a tad from all those super-romanticized ideas about motherhood. My whole mental balance was off-kilter and in those first twelve months, it really hit home how difficult I found it to ask for help. I very badly wanted to be able to manage and do everything myself. And as a result, I was soon at the end of my tether, with a husband who kept on asking what he could do to help me, only to hear me answer, "Oh no, it's okay, I'm fine, I've got this!" I had plenty of people who wanted to help, but usually I simply didn't let them. And the weird thing is that it had nothing to do with me being afraid they would do it wrong. It was all fine; they could put the clean diaper on her head and let her take a nap in the dog crate, for all I cared. My inability to accept help wasn't because I was too controlling. It was more that I felt like I'd be asking too much, since the baby was first and foremost my responsibility. Um, yes, now that you mention it, I'm the sort of person that prefers to tidy up before the cleaning lady comes. And motherhood was no different. "It's all right, let me do it. After all, I made the kid too," I'd repeat over and over. Until I was so exhausted it just wasn't doable anymore. I had to seriously crash into that wall before I finally decided to stop listening to the little voice from the past that kept saying, "You have to do it all yourself, Kel." Since then, I've changed that into, "Yes, I'm perfectly capable of doing it all myself, but it's nice to have help. Many hands make light work, right?!"

Everyone has their own parenthood challenges. When I'd hear parents talk about being insecure, I realized I didn't struggle with that anymore. Models are scrutinized under a microscope, and I also think ending certain friendships has really helped me develop more self-esteem. So I've never bothered with questions like, "Am I doing it right? Am I a good mother? Does my child lack for nothing?" or, "How in the world does *she* manage it all?!" I'd usually quickly tell myself, "I'm doing the best I can and I give a lot of love. Yes, I'm bound to make mistakes, but I'm a good mother in my own way." What I did struggle with was asking for help, creating more balance, being overstimulated and trying to not completely disregard myself.

Every new mother needs to learn that everyone has their own way of managing motherhood. I didn't have anyone in my immediate vicinity with recent parenting experience, and the people outside this inner circle were the sort who made it seem like it was child's play. Well, it might have been easy for them, but for me... not so much. Of course there were also seventh-heaven moments, when I had my baby girl in my arms, breastfeeding, the house all peaceful and quiet, and I'd fondle her hair and bury my nose in that velvety neck of hers. Yes, at moments like that, everything felt perfect. And it was perfect. But at the same time we're also talking mile-long maternity pads, mastitis, months of hardly sleeping, a completely new relationship dynamic, suddenly having an infant present that needs constant attention, and how the fuck to find the time to so much as take a shower, let alone run a business!?

It definitely took some adjustment. And the beauty of it all is that you do it. You manage. And the most beautiful about it, is that you'd do it all over again in a heartbeat. The most beautiful things in life are sometimes also the most challenging, that's a simple fact. Being pregnant, becoming a mother, being a mother – it's one big learning process. I knew myself, knew who I was, but in this all-encompassing new role, I had to set out in search of the new me. I had to figure out how to stay true to my inner self. Well, one way to definitely *not* do that is by comparing yourself to other people. It won't improve your personal development, nor your love life, nor your friendships or career, let alone motherhood. Again, it's all about checking in with yourself. "What do I need? What is my way of doing this?"

"

Life gets
so much *easier* if you
just stop explaining
yourself and
do whatever works
FOR YOU.

"

Being a mother has been the most beautiful thing in the world for me, but I also find it incredibly taxing, and saying that often feels like I'm saying something you're not supposed to say out loud. As if it means I don't love my kids or am ungrateful. "Oh, I would do anything for my children," was a reaction I'd sometimes get. Or: "You wouldn't say that if you hadn't been able to have kids." At moments like that, I'd think, "Girl, you don't have a clue who you're talking to and where I'm coming from." You know, as human beings, and certainly from one mother to another, we really should stop this whole thing of judging each other. Everyone has the right to live and experience their lives the way they want to. So what if I'm fed up with playing at make-believe with Barbies?! So what if I don't feel like cooking yet another healthy meal they won't touch anyway?! So what if I'm fucking exhausted!? Don't worry, it's not like I'm going to sell the kids on eBay! I'm allowed to struggle with the parts that are hard for me. If someone else has a different opinion, fine, let them, they're totally allowed to. But please, let's stop badgering each other about stuff like that.

Sometimes I really wonder how much better we'd all feel if we'd just keep our mouths shut a little more often. To decide that this time we won't immediately express an opinion. To not immediately share our standpoint on this issue. As an introvert, I find talking for the sake of talking pretty draining anyway. If I have nothing valuable to contribute to a conversation, I'd much rather stay quiet, and just listen. But sometimes it feels like we're supposed to have an opinion about everything and everyone nowadays. As if we have to share and discuss absolutely everything – and choose sides, too. Even if you're clueless about the whole subject! Sounds exhausting, right?

When I became a mother, all this meddling in other people's lives became all too visible. If there's anything that has improved my life, it's having learned to look at situations from a distance. To not immediately react from emotion but to first ask myself, "What do I really think of this? And what do I really want here?" Because you have a choice: to respond, to listen or to let it go. And in this era of total overstimulation, I can't tell you how wonderful it is to not to let yourself get riled up by everything and everyone. Seriously, it does wonders. It's a great boost for your energy levels and peace of mind. Since becoming a mother, I've discovered I don't have an opinion about all sorts of matters anymore, and I like it that way.

*

I think comparing is the root of all evil, especially regarding motherhood. The always-greener grass at the neighbors' and all that. Sooooo many women look at other women and wonder, "Am I doing it the right way? Am I a good mother? A nice woman? A dear friend? Maybe I'm working too much?" Yeah, well, very generous and all, but why not try thinking about yourself a tad more. "What do I think is important? What do I need? Am I doing just fine in my own eyes?" Those are the questions I ask myself to keep choosing what makes me happy. Because constantly doing things that don't make you happy definitely won't make you a nicer partner or a dearer friend, and it sure as hell won't make you a better mother. Whether you choose to invest in your career or to stay at home for the kids, decide to curl up on the couch with a book to recharge instead of meeting up with a friend for a drink, or do decide to go out together and paint the town red – all of it should be geared towards your happiness. The number-one insight that has given me enormous peace of mind is that there isn't just one correct way to lead your life, nor a one and only way to be a mother. There is only the way that works for you. Dare to choose!

66

I've been tired in ways I didn't even know were possible, and still, I've always found the energy to get up again. Breastfeeding, reading books, wiping bottoms, making sandwiches – whenever you asked for mommy, I'd be there. Complaining that I really missed having some me-time, but not allowing myself to actually have it, because I couldn't stand the thought of missing you. Even when I'm at my worst, all I have to do is look at your sleeping faces at night to feel my very best again. There are often times I have no idea what I'm doing, and yet I always know exactly what you need. Other opinions don't matter; my intuition has never been so strong. You are the cause of permanent chaos in my home, but you also bring me peace of mind. And when your tiny hands grab mine, I'm so unbelievably proud, and convinced that I will never feel this proud about anything else in my life. Already so big, but still so small. Being your mom is an immense responsibility, but without a doubt, the greatest gift of all.

99

Due to all the choices you have to make, feeling guilty takes on a whole new meaning when you become a mother. For me it felt like there were tons of expectations out there and always in a few too many different areas, so that I would constantly think I was cutting corners and coming up short. I'm guessing almost every mother recognizes the feeling that there's always someone who wants something from you, whether it's your child, partner, friends, work, family or society as a whole. Oh, and let's not forget ourselves! And the result? Mom guilt, with all these mothers feeling bad that they sometimes do drop the ball. Come on, that doesn't make sense at all! We're setting the bar so unbelievably high. And why? Perfect doesn't exist. Seriously! There isn't just one correct way of doing things, but a thousand and one or more. And option A isn't necessarily better than option B. Striving to achieve the 'best way' is an unattainable goal. It's a recipe for failure. *Well, helloooooo, stress!* It's not about how somebody else does it. Ask yourself, "How do I want to do it?" Please accept that motherhood – and life in general – is an exercise in trial and error and that you're allowed to make mistakes. It will make your life so much more relaxed and realistic. Children don't need a perfect mom, they need someone who gives them loads of love: who when she's there, is *really* there.

A mom who feels good about herself because she hasn't forgotten she also needs to take good care of herself.

With every challenge in life, I try to figure out what it can teach me. My children have given my life a very clear focus. They are my number-one priority and lots of other things have suddenly become a lot less important as a result. Thanks to them, I find it even easier to make choices and set priorities. One of the things I no longer expect from myself is successfully juggling everything at once. I can't do that; nobody can. No one can excel at everything, so stop trying to be a wonder woman. Just start making choices! "What is my priority right now? What is important for my happiness right now? What or who do I need to achieve this?" And the rest of those balls? For now, just let them drop to the floor. For me, as a mother, making choices has definitely been an important theme. I no longer ask myself "How can I do everything?" and instead ask, "What am I going to stop doing?" For me, that's where happiness lies.

*

Parents can talk until they're blue in the face, but in the end kids always end up copying their parents' behavior. Don't underestimate the power of role models. What you *say* goes in one ear and out of the other, but they will absolutely imitate what you *do*. I myself don't have a specific parenting style, but I do try to be a good role model and set a good example. So I pay extra attention to demonstrating what I appreciated so much in my own upbringing: the family bond, hard work, the no-nonsense attitude, humor and self-deprecation, gratitude, being caring and considerate, and never ever feeling too superior for anything or anyone.

I also try to help them avoid the pitfalls I stepped into, and to raise them to be self-sufficient and give them the space to ask for help as well. We don't say ugly things about ourselves, our bodies or our achievements. And yes, we are down-to-earth, but there's room for emotions as well. We cuddle every day and I've noticed I frequently tell them "I'm so proud of you!" or "Well done!" Not that I want to raise little narcissists, because I also tell them what they didn't do well and have to work on. But I do want to be supportive. Parenthood is the perfect mirror for solving your own issues and making sure you burden your children as little as possible with your own baggage. The most beautiful thing you can do for them is to solve your own shit first, so they can just be themselves.

I guess I always try to strike a happy medium as a parent. Just like the essence of what I wrote in my previous two books, I try very hard to avoid black-and-white thinking and prefer to go for a pinch of salt and pepper. I'm a big fan of not making things too complicated and just letting it go whenever possible. On the other hand, it's sometimes smart to sink your teeth into a subject. I consider values and morals important. So I won't reward emotional blackmail from my kids. Like the notorious temper tantrums in the supermarket. Yes, it's awful if your kid puts you on the spot by going bananas, but one thing that is absolutely not going to happen is my kid getting the candy anyway, not after all that. Nope, I'm the sort of parent who sticks to her guns. Something I've really had to learn in life, is how to define and set boundaries, and I've totally mastered that. Too bad for my kids, since they can now no longer take advantage of that potential weakness!

I'm a big advocate of letting children discover their own identity within the framework I give them. They're allowed to find their own way, and I'll let them know beforehand if they're about to drive into the guard rail. Because besides the old-fashioned Dutch rule of parenting – rest, routine and cleanliness above all – I believe children thrive when they're given clear boundaries and have parents who are consistent in enforcing those. It gives children a sense of safety and predictability. Very pronounced choices in parenting are not my thing, and I don't have any illusion that I'd create perfect people that way either. All those kids who were raised completely sugar-free, screen-free, were breastfed, only ate organic food, received an anthroposophical education and co-slept with their parents until they were fifteen years old to ensure secure attachment... Well, my guess is that they will later on end up in the same bar as my kids, while downing shots and sneaking a smoke. They too are also going to rebel and will want to establish their own identity. All children are undoubtedly going to make their own mistakes, as they should. And yes, mine are undoubtedly going to do all sorts of stuff that isn't allowed according to my rules. And the more I forbid those or push them in a certain direction, the more interested they will be in exploring the tantalizing unknown. I am really aiming for a happy medium so as not to pressure them. Which is nice for them, and nice for me. I don't wonder how all the other moms go about it; instead, I simply ask myself, "How do I want to do this?" I'd rather not make things unnecessarily difficult.

*

Happiness is in the little things, and motherhood has given me the clarity to notice those every day. Time and again, I look at my girls, thinking 'so beautiful' to myself. My mom had two daughters, and now I have two daughters. The other day my mom said: "Isn't it nice how the girls interact with each other, without the slightest trace of jealousy. You two were the same, and you're still best friends." History repeats itself. And when I see them at moments like that, when they're playing and laughing together, only briefly pausing their play to give me a hug, I'm in seventh heaven.

When I look at my girls, I sincerely hope they will learn the same things I did in my youth. Unconditional love. Knowing I would never fall too deep, since there was always a safety net, but in the meantime also being allowed to make my own choices. It creates space to be yourself. Having the power of choice. It makes a huge difference for your self-esteem. Giving your children a healthy dose of self-confidence is a good antidote for many problems later on in life, problems that often originate in childhood. I support my girls through thick and thin. And like I said, children don't listen to what you say, they look at what you do. My biggest lesson is therefore: if I want them to be happy, I have to be happy. And that means not just talking about it, but showing them.

"

Ultimately, the most *beautiful* thing you can do for your kids is SOLVE YOUR OWN shit so they can just be themselves.

"

AMBITION

I graduated from high school on a pre-university track, I have a master's in psychology, and I was Miss Netherlands for a year. And I spent the next twelve years trying to get rid of that last label. Being in a relationship with a pretty well-known Dutch guy didn't exactly help either. Meanwhile, I've written three bestsellers and I have my own coaching practice and publishing company, so by now people luckily know I'm more about content than looks. But still, for a long time, I had the stifling urge to prove something to the world. Partly because I had to deal with the "Miss Netherlands" label for so long, which seemed to make people take my expertise less seriously. And partly because ever since childhood, people had always said I was so lucky. At first, I was told that I owed my success to my parents, then it was my looks, then it was my partner. "Some people have all the luck." Meanwhile, I was working my ass off – only too gladly, by the way – but no one ever said: "Wow, you did a great job, Kelly!" When something went well, I owed it to everyone and everything except my own dedication and hard work.

As I already mentioned in the chapter about my childhood, my earliest memories all involve working. Helping to feed the pigs on the farm, babysitting my cousins, helping out in the store, and from the age of 14 onwards, side hustling in cafés and restaurants every weekend. At a young age, I already noticed that not being lazy makes life more fun. Making your own money gives you freedom of choice. Creating your own wins builds self-confidence, because you feel proud and regularly get approving pats on the back. And I'm still convinced that in life overall, not being lazy is extremely useful. It helps you pull things off. It's nice to have talent, but work ethic and discipline will take you further. Putting my back into something is such an integral part of my identity – due to my DNA, my upbringing and all the ensuing beliefs – that without realizing it, I struggled enormously with the fact that people didn't always consider me a person who consistently goes the extra mile. As if everything just – *ta-da!* – magically fell into my lap.

Likewise, I've always been very aware of the fact that I'm a white woman living in the Western world and have been very fortunate to be born where I was, living a life of privilege, with the luxury of having so many more choices than other people get. So yes, I am a very lucky girl! And with that in the back of my mind, I guess I started believing the little voice that said "everything falls into your lap" just a *little* too much. Because it hit me right where it hurts, in that mental sore spot every person has, with the number-one question, "Am I worth it?" Like I said before, every human being wants to be valued and appreciated. And this need can trigger some pretty strange behavior.

Since I'm so ambitious and so sensitive to this issue, I was caught up in my own rat race to prove myself. For a long time, I kept rushing from one goal to the next. When I was a waitress, I wanted to have the highest earnings every day; when I was a model, I wanted to book the most jobs; when I participated in a beauty pageant, I wanted to become Miss Netherlands, and when I was a psychologist, I wanted to achieve the best results. Later on, when I wrote my first book, I decided the highest possible achievement would be for it to be a bestseller – and it was. Did I take the time to truly enjoy it? Nope. I started working on my second book almost immediately. I've always felt the pressure to race on. But who was pressuring me? Who said, "Oh, you should definitely write another book, Kel!" Yeah, okay, the publisher did kind of like the idea at the time, but I'm afraid I have to admit it was also just me. It was my own need to prove myself.

When you hammer it into your head that you should always keep going, moving right on to the next thing, and feel totally worthless whenever you take a break and cut yourself some slack – as if you're not contributing to society or are a waste of space – you will never really enjoy what you already have. Fortunately, these past years I've managed to pursue my ambition in a domain that makes me very happy, but I've spent precious little time on actually appreciating and enjoying everything I've achieved. The ambitious side of my character has probably brought me most in life, but posed the greatest challenges at the same time. I'm guessing this applies to most people: our biggest strength is often also our greatest pitfall.

*

I'm slowly embracing the insight that it's pretty smart to occasionally just play it by ear and see what happens. To do stuff without automatically linking it to a goal. I call that my 'Vegetable Garden Insight'. I'm the sort of person who sees one seed and thinks, "Nice! This has potential!" and then immediately wants to create a complete botanical garden. My Vegetable Garden Insight is that I need to sow that one seed and take pleasure in that, since it's also about enjoying the process itself, feeling like a pig in clover while I'm working, and deriving satisfaction from that. I don't need to jump straight to focusing on how many fruit baskets it might yield, thus immediately setting the bar so high for myself again. As a result, I go over the top and switch into hyperdrive mode right away. And if I find out that for some reason it's not doable... Okay, fine, then just forget about it!

Yes, I know it's dumb, but that's just the way I am. If I want to tidy up my closet, I can't just do one shelf at a time. No, I leave it cluttered, and then once I start, the whole damn thing needs to be tidied in one go. The junk ends up in a pile on the floor and the rest is neatly arranged by color and season. And since I want to do something good as well, I also prepare several bags to donate to charity, all at the same time. This is just an example of the selective perfectionist side I have in me, because I have no problem whatsoever pulling the door of the exploded laundry room shut behind me to take the girls to the playground. That's because I go all the way for captivating activities that I care about. And in the end, this attitude brings me a lot of good as well.

It's one of the reasons that although I'm only 33

years old, I have so many things in my life sorted out. I've absolutely had a lot of luck in life, but I've also worked fucking hard to get where I am. This deep intrinsic motivation of mine means I not only want to be a wonderful mom and a great partner, but competent and successful in my work as well. And I don't believe in cutting corners. This attitude gives me energy, but also takes a lot of effort. I'm totally capable of geeing myself up. And then invariably end up asking myself, "Why am I doing this?!" Well, because it's worth it!

Will I continue to race on and on? Like, do I want an even larger family? Do I want to help even more people? Report even higher earnings? Get yet another degree? I realize I shouldn't keep going in autopilot mode. My foundation is rock solid. And now *would* be a good time to stop and smell the roses. What I definitely don't want to do anymore is to be tripped up by the pitfall of having to somehow prove myself, or associate having time off with feeling worthless. Getting recognition is great, but only when *I'm* proud of it too.

"

DREAMS are often much more realistic than *you* think. You just need the courage to PURSUE them.

"

Who is it that I want to prove myself to? I think about that a lot. The answer I usually come up with is that I'm primarily proving it to myself. So then I tell myself: "You don't need anything from anyone, Kel! You're totally capable of validating yourself. You have nothing to prove. Let them think whatever they want to think." And I have more peace of mind now. Yes, it's been a whole process, but I've become so much better at it.

I'm so glad I've reached a point in my life that I'm using my ambition for the right things. No longer for what I think other people expect of me, or for something other people would consider 'just a dream', but for what I love and find fulfilling. People spend so much of their lives working that it can get tricky if you choose to do something you don't actually like all that much. If that happens, your private life sure has to have a *lot* on offer to be able to counterbalance that. It wasn't until college that I realized how much of what we decide to do is unintentionally chosen because our parents, friends or society in general expect it of us. Or maybe you even have those expectations yourself and were led to believe a particular high-profile job would make you happy, but in actual practice it turns out to be totally ill-suited for you.

I constantly try to ask myself the right questions.

I no longer wonder: "What's going to make other people happy? How can I impress them? How can I show I've worked hard for what I have?" Questions I should ask myself instead include: "Why do I think I have to prove myself? What do I have to prove anyhow?" Because unfortunately that other voice keeps piping up, the one seeking validation from other people. The one that says it's not fair. The one that is allergic to prejudice. The one that says: "Show me you can do it, prove it!" And unfortunately, that's my cue. That's just how it works in my brain. I needed to figure out how this process worked and learn to recognize it. We all have our psychological patterns, that's totally normal, but it is convenient to know that you have them. When you're aware of it, you can overcome those patterns or turn the volume of those voices down a bit. "What is my ambition and why do I want to do this for myself? Will it fulfill me? What do I want to achieve, and why? What does it bring me?" Those are the questions that helped me figure out what I *really* wanted, and to choose that more often. They also helped me figure out that this urge to prove myself was getting in my way, holding me back. Far too often, it was about convincing others, and deep down inside about convincing myself. Now I say to myself: "You're worth it, Kel. You're good the way you are. Now, in this moment. Nothing else and nothing extra is needed." At that point, it becomes so much less scary to fail and make mistakes, because your self-esteem no longer depends on the outcome or on other people's opinions.

*

So why did I decide I wanted to write an international bestseller? Because when I'm eighty years old I don't want to look back on my life and think "If only I had..." Not in my work, and not in my private life. If I spot an opportunity, something I'm excited about, I jump on it. I hear way too many people say that they have dreams and passions, but don't dare to pursue them because they're afraid of failure. Or people who give up too quickly because they failed once. It's such a shame, because hey, that's life! Nobody knows how to do everything in advance, without ever having done it. Nobody can achieve anything without occasionally falling flat on their face. So yes, you will encounter setbacks, you will fall. That's precisely how people learn and grow and eventually achieve what they want. The low points eventually lead to high points. And because of those lows, you will appreciate the highs all the more. You know, if I don't do anything, it sure as hell isn't going to be a success. And yes, if I do try to do something, there's the risk of failure, but it's 100% certain that it'll be a wonderful adventure. And if life has taught me anything, it's that every endeavor that starts off with "Fuck it, let's just do it!" weirdly enough usually turns out to be a success. Dreams are often so much more realistic than you think; you just have to have the courage to pursue them. Nothing ventured, nothing gained!

"But don't you feel guilty that you're so ambitious since you also have kids? And why do you work so hard for your career? It's not like you really need that with such a successful partner, right?" Those are actual questions I regularly get asked, and it always make me wonder how often working dads get asked the same thing. And since when is work only about the money? Yes, I do like to earn my own money, so the financial aspect is an important motive, but doing what I do also makes me really happy. It's something I need emotionally. I've always been ambitious, even when I was very young. I simply need to work! I really *want* to be an entrepreneur. And yes, I also want to be an independent woman, financially too. It gives me peace of mind and the freedom to organize my life the way I want to. In my opinion, that doesn't suddenly vanish when a partner arrives on the scene. The same applies to the arrival of children, although I have made some changes for the sake of efficiency, since I also want to have enough time to spend with them. So no, I don't feel guilty at all about how I've organized things. Everyone tries to do what they deem best for their brood. And fortunately, there are lots of different ways to be a good parent, whether you work full-time, are a stay-at-home parent, or anything in between.

I'm passionate about my work and am convinced I'm a more loving mother because I continue to make room for my professional hopes and dreams. Moreover, motherhood has made me a better entrepreneur, and my being an entrepreneur makes me a better mother! I think it's important to show my daughters that their daddy is not the only one with a career. I want to raise strong women who can hold their own. Besides, they aren't missing out on anything, since all their creature comforts are taken care of, including a great babysitter and good times spent with grandma. I have a lot of quality time with them myself. So why should I feel guilty when they're having fun while I'm at work during the day? When I was on maternity leave, I did of course wonder whether I was a good mother whenever I also made time for work, but it's actually a stupid question. What makes me happy? That's the question I should be wondering about. Well, I certainly don't want to abandon my own sense of joy in life simply because

I have children – not in my work and not in life in general – but instead I have chosen to organize things in such a way that I have time for myself as well as for them. I think my ambition sets a good example for them, to help them pursue their own dreams later on in their life. Whatever those dreams may be.

*

At what time in my life did I feel out of balance? When I was constantly doing stuff that wasn't really my thing. So much so that it stopped giving me energy. I directed my drive into modeling, being Miss Netherlands, studying law, maintaining a huge group of friends and a much too busy social life – but in retrospect, my heart wasn't in any of those things. Balance remains a continuous concern, since ambition is such an integral part of who I am. And not only in my work, but in all areas of my life. In the end, being ambitious boils down to wanting to excel. And excelling is what I want to do with all the things I'm juggling all the time.

On Sunday night, I always look at my calendar – reviewing the past week and planning for the next one. What did I do, what are my plans for the coming week, and what does my schedule look like? Does it fill me with dread, or do I immediately find myself looking forward to it? Do I have time for myself, or does it look like I might already be completely stressed out halfway through the week? If necessary, I tackle it right away, by canceling something and scheduling in some me-time. After all, practice what you preach, right? What to choose and what not to. In the end, the power of choice is all about 'feeling in balance'. What do you spend your time on? Many people don't plan at all, they just react to whatever comes along. They don't make clear choices themselves and so their schedule becomes something that 'happens' to them. Balance starts with taking (back) control, and that starts with your schedule. What do you say yes to and what do you say no to?

Everyone struggles with their work-life balance. At work we're missing out on things at home, but at home we're missing out on career opportunities. Maintaining this balance remains a challenge for me as well, but planning effectively and learning to say no is a good start. Ask yourself: "What are a few things or people that are preventing me from achieving a better balance? What do I really want to do now, and what do I definitely not want to do? What do I really want to do when I'm off work? What gives me energy? What doesn't give me energy? Is it nice enough to reserve time for? Do I care enough about it to make time for it? What do I really think is important?" It can get complicated, since so many things are possible. What should we choose when there is so much to choose from? People think happiness is derived from all the things we say yes to, but it's actually more the result of what we say no to.

*

I'm always telling myself I have to do all sorts of things. Due to how I'm wired, combined with the no-nonsense way I was raised, I'm only allowed to enjoy myself after 'earning' it. I have to make good use of my time. To first put in the work if I want something. To have crossed off everything on my to-do list. There's nothing inherently wrong with any of that. Like I said, it has also brought me a lot. But yes, you can overdo it... So I now ask myself more often: "Who am I doing this for? Why do I want to achieve this? What do I have to prove? When is it enough?" Because what I do know by now is this: even if you work your way through the whole to-do list, there's always more. Even if you've worked day in day out to accomplish something, people are still going to say you've just been lucky and it simply fell into your lap. And even if you go all out for somebody else, it simply will never be enough for some people.

In the meantime, I've received a bit of recognition, although of course everything is relative. My work is not worthy of a Nobel Prize, but I'm glad I've managed to reach a reasonable amount of people with my expertise and have had a positive impact. If I – God forbid – get hit by a bus tomorrow, my last thought won't be, "Oh, but it's so terrific that I wrote a bestseller." Although my life's center of gravity lies elsewhere, I absolutely love my work. There have been lots of reasons for breaking out the champagne. Like when I accomplish a professional milestone. That's a moment to cherish and enjoy. It's a reward. And then, the moment is over. It's time to put things into their proper perspective again, because those victories are a nice bonus, but they're not what's most important to me. I would hate it if, when I'm not around anymore, people would say: "Jeez, she always worked so hard! What a great career." So what?! I'd rather have them say: "She was a wonderful mother and a very dear friend. She was there for me when I needed her. Her work really helped me a lot. Oh my god, we had so much fun together. We really had the best time ever!" Now *that's* what I would love to hear. So that's why I keep asking myself, "Why do I do what I do?" It's a good question I think everyone should ask themselves every now and then. "What is it that fulfills me?"

I will always be ambitious. The more R&R I get, the more ideas I come up with. I simply have entrepreneurial blood flowing through my veins and really do see potential business opportunities everywhere and in everything. I've also noticed that I usually manage to make it into a success, because I fire on all cylinders to succeed. No matter how often I fall flat on my face, I always get up again and look for a new way to get it done. So yeah, I dream big because I like to. I love to mull over things like conquering the world with my books and my coaching practice, setting up another company and doing something totally different in an area that interests me – and believe me, I've got plenty of those. I never think, "Oh, I would never be able to do that," when someone else manages to accomplish something that I haven't done yet. No, it actually motivates me. If that other person can do it, then so can I!

What I have started to do is to write those thoughts down and let them just sit there for a while. (And sometimes I just let it simmer in my head.) The challenge is to set goals, but also allow myself enough rest, and to only do those things I really want to spend my time and energy on. To pursue my ambitious hopes and dreams with what really fulfills me and gives me joy and pleasure. I am ambitious, but I don't have anything to prove anymore, not to others and not to myself. And that feels good.

"

You have NOTHING
to prove. Just let
them think *whatever*
they want.

"

LOSS

I'd known Dennis since we were kids. When we were little, his parents also spent their summer vacations in Spain and the two of us would have a blast. He was always full of energy, truly the life and soul of a party. But as these things go, time passed, we got older, and I went off to study in the Dutch equivalent of the Deep South, while he stayed in the urban, western part of the country. As a result, we lost contact. But at some point during my travels all over the world, we met up again in New York City, where he'd moved to pursue his language studies. And we just picked up where we left off. We explored the city together, went out on the town and were sometimes hardly able to walk because we'd be laughing so hard.

And then came November 10th, 2013. He was back in Holland, driving home from work at two o'clock in the morning. He was on the freeway when a person driving on the wrong side of the road came out of nowhere. He couldn't avoid her; it was a head-on collision. When I woke up that morning, I saw loads of missed calls and text messages. It was horrifying news. He was gone forever. Twenty-four years old and in the prime of his life. Snatched away by a drunk driver on the wrong side of the road, who had survived the crash.

The funeral made a huge impression on me, attended by hundreds of people, many my own age. How could this have happened to 'one of us'? These kinds of things shouldn't happen. It wasn't right. From one moment to the next, he was no longer there. What if he had headed home just a few minutes later? Why did this have to happen to him? "What if...?" and "Why?" were questions I asked myself over and over in the following months. Want to feel absolutely awful? Just keep asking yourself those questions over and over. Because you're not going to get a satisfying answer. Not ever. Not an answer that would make you think, "Oh! Okay then, fine!"

Is there a better way to deal with awful things like this? Well, I will never forget what his mother told me: "The worst thing in my life has already happened. I'm no longer afraid of anything anymore. All the time I have left here is an added bonus, and I want to enjoy that time. He wouldn't have wanted it any different."

What an exemplary response, to be able to react like that to something so horrific. What an eye-opener! I'm not afraid of death itself, but I do fear it might come too soon. It's my biggest fear, dying while my daughters are still small. Or even worse: losing your child. Which is what happened to her. The very worst twist of fate, but she was exceptionally able to let go of something that she had no agency over. She decided to focus purely on what was within the scope of her control – without asking questions like "Why?" or "What if?", but instead learning to live with how everything was now. Every day is new and the trick is to seize those moments.

*

People can be terribly unfortunate in life. Take Dennis. Or another friend of ours, Igor. He was ill, suffering from bipolar disorder. Sometimes I would want to shout at him: "Please enjoy life! Look at what you do have! There are so many people who love you! So many adventures still await you!" But I know that's naïve. Sometimes people feel like they're stuck in a deep, dark hole and it's a genetic thing that they're no longer capable of feeling the power of choice. To them, everything is dark and dismal. Please remember that suicide isn't a cowardly act.

Not at all! Imagine the guts you need to have to be able to do that. It's terrifying and lonely. And it just goes to show how difficult life must be for someone to think that the alternative – death – would seem like a better option.

Until then, I'd only experienced loss from a distance. When my grandpa died, I was too young to really get it. And now death was suddenly so close, and in ways I'd never expected – ways I didn't consider 'normal'. It made me sad, but strangely also led to appreciation, perspective and insight. Especially the realization that death really is a part of life and that it's better to avoid saying, "Oh yeah, I'll do that, but not today." The question you should be asking yourself the whole time is rather: "Why not now?!" Go on, do it! Don't wait. Dare to choose. Seize those moments. Allow yourself enough rest, put the laptop away to have fun and chill out, because you don't fully appreciate what you have. I've gotten better and better at that.

So how do I cope with grief? Well, not by asking myself, "What is the right way to do this?" One of my mantras has become "How do I want to process grief?" Losing someone is complicated, and the opinions and views about it verge on the absurd. The idea that someone should be over it by now, or is moving on too fast, grieving too openly, enjoying life too blatantly, has a small altar in their house to remember their loved one, never visits the grave... As if there's a universal handbook for mourning, an officially approved way to grieve. Bullshit! You can only do what feels right for you. It became easier for me to find closure by not worrying about how other people grieve and just feeling how I want to do it. Therapy can be a wonderful way to process grief if you feel like you're drowning in sadness, but in my work, with my friends and family, as well as in my own personal experience, I've noticed the trick is to give yourself time. You'll often manage to figure out how to deal with it as long as you don't force yourself to do things in a certain way, dictated by external opinions.

I've discovered sadness can be pretty darn scary. I can easily put it on hold and give it a positive twist, and I sometimes compare it to the ocean. Usually it's just calm, rippling waves, nothing out of the ordinary, until a storm suddenly picks up, whipping the waves so high that you almost drown. And in the end, you can never be entirely sure what the weather will be like; you can only learn to swim well enough to be prepared.

Two years after Igor's death, John and I went to see the movie *A Star Is Born*, starring Lady Gaga and Bradley Cooper. He gets depressed and in one of the last scenes, he decides to end his life. Right before that, he feels so incredibly lonely and so totally worthless that he doesn't want to be a burden to anyone anymore. And somehow that hit me terribly hard. I broke down and started crying. And I mean like really ugly-crying. I was almost hyperventilating and just couldn't stop anymore. I was still crying when the movie was over, bawling my eyes out in the parking lot and continuing in the car home. I fell apart completely, but felt super relieved afterwards. I guess I still needed some closure. Everyone has their own way of getting there. And those moments usually aren't something you can schedule in. Sometimes they simply appear out of nowhere, even when you thought you'd left it all behind.

I do know it doesn't help if I get stuck in sadness. I choose not to ignore it, but to face it head-on and to keep going. I mean, come on – if you're going through hell, you're not going to stop there, right? For me the trick is to not focus on all the things that are no longer there, on what is no longer possible, on the circumstances of what happened (so unfair!), on the injustice of it all. Not that I'm in denial, but we shouldn't forget to look at the other side of the coin. What *did* I have? What *am* I still able to do? What do I actually think about death? What can losing someone teach me? And how can death make me appreciate life more? Loss and grief have helped me put things into perspective even more. Which is not the same as downplaying it, because I acknowledge my emotions. But I do now manage to get unstuck sooner, instead of dwelling on irrelevant crap or on things I can't change anyway. Once you've experienced something extremely sad or awful, you spend so much less time worrying about the things that aren't all that bad.

"

GRIEF is
love that can
no longer be shared.
It's THE LOVE you
want to give, but the
person *you* want
to give it to is no
longer around.

"

Loss made me more spiritual. Dennis' death played a big role in that. When Dennis died, Pharrell Williams' song "Happy" was at the top of the charts. It was played at his funeral, as a way of commemorating and celebrating how joyous his life had been. And it's uncanny how often I'll be thinking of him, in the car for instance, and suddenly the radio will start playing exactly that song. And by that I mean that I won't even have the radio on, but it suddenly switches on by itself, and starts playing that exact same song! It always happens like that, and in that order: first I think of him, and then suddenly I hear that specific song somewhere.

The other day I was working in a coffee place in the village where we live. I had actually just started on this chapter and was writing about Dennis. They had some kind of 80's playlist, featuring Spandau Ballet, Wham! and so on. And then suddenly the first notes of "Happy" blared out of the speakers. What the fuck?! A similar thing happened when John and I were watching the movie *Interstellar*. We'd already seen it and we don't usually watch a movie twice, but that night, I felt a strange urge that I needed to watch it again. In a couple of scenes, Morse code plays a significant role. It's how the main character tries to establish contact with his family on Earth. And we're sitting there watching the movie and out of the blue, the air conditioning in the room started making a weird sort of rattling and ticking sound. John burst out laughing. "Hey, it even sounds a bit like Morse code!" He thought it was hilarious and wanted to decipher it, just for fun. But when he looked it up, I could tell from the expression on his face that something was off. Guess what the Morse code spelled out? I.g.o.r. "Yeah right! Like I believe that!" I cried out. When the air conditioning started rattling again, I took out my phone to record it so I could decipher it for myself. Again: I.G.O.R. This was nuts! If we hadn't been watching that movie right then, we would never have thought of Morse code! And now it was like he wanted to let us know he was there. Sooooo weird!

Later that week, we were having dinner in a restaurant on Ibiza, one of those places where they only play lounge music. And all of a sudden we heard the song from his funeral coming out of the speakers. "Four Seasons in One Day", the song he used to play on his guitar. And immediately after that, the same song again, but this time sung by a woman. Come on, nobody makes that kind of playlist! And sure, it could all be a coincidence, but I don't believe that. I think it's a sign from the universe, maybe even from him in some way. And I think that's beautiful; it consoles me. And there are countless similar incidents, none of them as random as something like a butterfly flapping its wings – although that also happens pretty often. Sometimes I'll say, "Hi there, grandma," chuckling and thinking to myself, "Right, this is total nonsense." But an air conditioner that starts to emit Morse code?! Now that's a first.

My explanation for all of this is that things happen without us being able to grasp it, because our senses aren't equipped to process it. But these things do exist. Just like dolphins communicate and hunt via sonar. Humans can't hear it, because our ears can't pick up that frequency. But that doesn't mean it doesn't exist, does it? I think that death is death; it's final and we should find our peace in that. But it's comforting to sometimes pick up something that helps you find that peace. Ultimately, I guess this too is a choice. You can either ignore it and think it's total nonsense, or you can choose to think there is someone behind it, maybe guided by your own wish. This second option regularly brings a smile to my face and inspires me to briefly stop and think about a beautiful memory of someone I miss. So that's what I choose to believe. It's my way of finding closure. To now and then have the feeling that the person I miss is reaching out to me.

I think I would describe myself as a down-to-earth spiritual person. I also consult a medium now and then. Many people are surprised when they hear this, but it's actually not at all out of character for me. In my view, being down-to-earth and being spiritual go hand in hand. Intuition, gut instinct – that's totally me! But rational thinking and logical reasoning are also me. Every human being has a primordial body made up of cells that have learned all kinds of things during millions of years. Why would we want to drown that out by thinking purely rationally? I always try to get the facts straight in my head, but I also make sure I know how I feel about a particular person or decision. I always factor that into my decision-making process. We humans have become so matter-of-fact that being attuned to our feelings has been snowed under – even though spirituality is completely logical when you believe in science. It's a proven fact that having a bad or a good feeling about something can be difficult to explain, but is definitely rooted in intellect. There's a reason that people are sometimes terrified of very deep, high or tight spaces. Those fears are almost never based on any past experience in their own lives. No, it's what evolved in our cells, after millions of years of previous experiences and the need to survive. This primal instinct tells us, "Noooo, not a good idea, enough of your ancestors plummeted off mountains, so let's prevent you from doing the same." That's also what our intuition tells us when we meet someone and think, "Hm, this doesn't feel quite right," or when you find yourself in a situation where your intuition is telling you: "Get out of here, now!" We have intuitive superpowers without being aware of it. We should really learn to listen to it.

So yeah, I sometimes consult a medium, because I kind of like to have my gut feeling spiritually confirmed. Confirmed by a person who can make contact with something I may not yet fully understand, but that I am brave enough to rely on. The best choices I've made in life were all based on intuition long before my brain could catch up. That held true every single time, whether the situation involved love, friendships, motherhood or a business decision. If something doesn't feel right, I won't do it. The times that somebody immediately gave me bad vibes? Later, that feeling always turned out to have been correct. I'm not saying that basing your whole day-to-day life on intuition is a good idea. No, it's good to keep thinking rationally, but please do listen to your instincts whenever you're about to embark on something new and exciting. More often than not, in that first split second you will know it's the best decision ever. Even before – or even without – being able to explain it rationally.

*

Although losing loved ones has taught me that life can often be incredibly unfair, the spiritual aspects of experiencing loss have left me more convinced than ever that what goes around, comes around. I try to be very aware of how I look at the world around me. To realize I can make clearcut choices based on an optimistic, positive outlook. I absolutely believe the universe gives you back what you throw into it. Not that I would go so far as to say to someone: "Ah, you have cancer? Well, did you know you can think yourself sick but also think yourself better?" No, I don't believe that at all. Nor do I believe that everything happens for a reason. It's disrespectful to people who really are ill and have truly horrible experiences. Bad luck is everywhere. And it's fucking brutal that we don't get any say in a lot of misery and hardship. I do, however, think it helps to have a positive mindset when going through something like that. Let's not dismiss it as flaky nonsense. I'm actually convinced we'll stop calling it that once science comes up with new facts. Then it will suddenly be called psychology or quantum mechanics or physics or mathematics. I really believe the ability to direct our thoughts and our focus will become the perfect tool for personal progress. When you tell yourself day in, day out that you're ill, it does something to you. If you tell yourself day in, day out "I'm healthy, I'm whole," you will not only start feeling that, but research shows that it also does something at a cellular level. So to a certain extent we can heal ourselves a little bit. Just like we also create our own reality to a large extent. It's something countless studies have proven, but I'd need another book to fully explain that passion of mine. What I'd like to stress is that it's very important to realize we don't see the world as it is, but as we are. Throwing positivity and love at yourself and the rest of the world absolutely impacts your life. Become the change you want to see.

"

Just because
you CARRY IT WELL
doesn't mean it
isn't *heavy.*

"

So yes, I want to have a positive outlook on life. I'd rather not think in doom scenarios. I'm not going to get any happier thinking things like "Why them and not me?" or "Why is this happening to me?" or "I hope they don't succeed." People who constantly trip up others, point out their mistakes, are resentful, primarily take instead of giving as well, or who are habitual liars – it's all dangerous. Stay away from that kind of mindset. And fix whatever is causing it. Besides the fact that I wish others the best of luck, I also think I myself am worthy of it. Similarly, I believe I'm tempting fate when I exhibit this kind of behavior myself. And sometimes that manifests itself in super-silly ways. Like when I've gone to the grocery store and have a ton of bags hanging all over the stroller, and have two children and a dog with me, only to discover I've forgotten to scan the package of rice at the self-service checkout. Even though it only costs 39 cents, I go back to pay for it, even if it means having to go all the way back to the other side of the village. I'm not sure if it's superstition, but I prefer to choose to do the right thing instead of having an outstanding debt to the universe. I have the choice to do right and throw love at the world, and I'm convinced that makes life more beautiful. I will find exactly what I look for in the world, so when I look for all sorts of positive things, I'm going to find those.

*

In 2021, my grandmother died. She had lived a good, full life; she was 94 years old, a beautiful age. It was the first 'normal' loss in my adult life. She was old and passed away quietly in her sleep, nothing abrupt or traumatic. It didn't feel unfair, which made a big difference in terms of grief. Of course I miss her, precisely because we were able to enjoy each other's company for so long and created so many memories together. But I'm at peace with her death, in the sense of: "This is okay, this is how it's meant to go."

But a child who falls ill or dies, unexpected accidents, illnesses that have a detrimental effect on mental or physical well-being, *those* things aren't supposed to happen. I find it so much more difficult to deal with those kinds of losses, because it somehow goes against my idea of 'how the world should be'. But see, that's the thing: the loss I've experienced has made me realize that life is indeed unfair. We shouldn't even assume that after being put out to grass, we will pass away peacefully in our own beds at the age of 80, in the presence of our loved ones. I'm not saying we should live in fear that something bad could happen to ourselves or to somebody we know. But do please let yourself feel gratitude that you're here and alive, right now. And your loved ones as well! Hacking your happiness is all about learning lessons from loss, embracing life every single day and truly turning it into a party.

Suppose you knew your days were counted. What would you do? Or, in a nutshell: what really, really matters? What do you want most from life? I think about that a lot. Because I want to be conscious of that right now. I want to live with feelings of gratitude at this time in my life. And my answer always boils down to this: all of the choices I've made were chosen so I would have enough quality time with my loved ones. So that we can make loads of memories together. So whatever choices I make in the future, having quality time with them is a must. Loss has taken dear people away from me, but I have gained so much as well. It doesn't mean I wouldn't rather have had those people here with me now, but you can't always choose what comes your way. You can, however, choose how you want to deal with what life throws at you. I appreciate life itself so much more than before. Not that the sorrow necessarily diminished over the years, but my life around it expanded. We don't outgrow it, but life grows around it. By being more aware of death, I'm able to enjoy every little bit of life I'm given so much more intensely. I feel grateful.

66

The feeling
of *loss remains.*
It doesn't shrink with
time, IT'S OUR LIFE
around it that
becomes larger.

99

GRATITUDE

Kel, think about this for a minute! There are currently 850 million people who don't have access to fresh drinking water. People who have to walk for miles and miles to the nearest well, and miles back again too, to provide water for their family every single day. And here I just have to turn on the faucet and wow, the water pours right out! When I'm in one of my complaining rants, wallowing in discontent, I confront myself with this simple fact. I don't do it often, because that's not really in my nature, but I don't mind behaving like that every once in a while. However, when I do get stuck in this kind of mood, it can be slightly frustrating. So that little water story is how I remind myself to think, "Okay, and now it's time to be grateful for what you have!"

I'm not a big fan of the gratitude mumbo-jumbo that the online #blessed mafia bombards us with. And I'm certainly not a die-hard monk. When I stub my toe on the corner of a table, I don't think, "Oh, but I'm sooooo grateful for these two feet of mine and the fact that I can walk on this beautiful Earth." No, I respond by swearing like a trooper. When the girls have had too much sugar, are completely hyper and so overstimulated that they can't stop shouting at each other, what definitely doesn't spring to mind are thoughts like, "Jeez, I feel so grateful for being able to hear these children's voices." When I drop a glass and it breaks, I usually carry on about it with relish until the very last shard is in the trash can. And when someone close to me falls ill, I don't think: "I'm so grateful for this life lesson."

People don't have to go through life in a constant state of gratitude. It's totally healthy to occasionally be very annoyed, complain about something or unleash a couple swear words. Because you usually feel better afterwards. It also makes it so much easier to deal with small and large setbacks. Seriously! For years now, I've justified my pretty smart-ass comments by referring to the results of a famous scientific study where people had to put their hand in a bucket of ice water and try to keep it submerged as long as possible. In one session they were instructed to be quiet, while in the other they were allowed to curse and yell. Well, guess what? When people are allowed to vocalize the pain, their pain tolerance goes up and they can stand the cold a lot longer. In short, occasionally losing your cool can feel good, although to keep life fun, it's smart to know when it's time to move on. To also remember to look at the flip side. What *is* going well? And what are you happy with? Gratitude, in other words.

I consider myself to be fairly materialistic. I like beautiful stuff, good food and luxurious vacations, especially when I'm able to share it with loved ones. The good thing is I really don't mind having to work my ass off to have enough money for all those things. And it's a very deliberate choice to spend it on those things, since I'm well aware of what I've had to do for it *or* deprive myself of. But yes, I do like my creature comforts. And I think it's bullshit when people say money doesn't make you happy; that's rich people talk. Because having money to spend sure makes life a lot easier, and so many nice things in life do come with a price tag. Besides, not having enough money for basic necessities is extremely stressful; in itself, that can cause misery. However, most people reading this are in the fortunate position of easily being able to meet those basic needs. And yet many of us continue to strive for more and more, or bigger, more expensive, more spectacular and just plain better, thinking it will make them even happier. But that's a fallacy, a pitfall that I have also fallen into a little too often. I'm sure you have a pretty good idea of how ambitious I am by now, and let me tell you: it didn't matter whether I achieved an even higher turnover, exceeded my target for the number of clients, managed to write a bestseller, wrote another bestseller, bought a bigger car or a nicer purse, none of it made me any happier. Sure, it was nice, but it didn't make me *happy*. If I were to make a list of what does make me happy, it would be things that I notice and experience every day, which usually – wow, who knew? – don't cost a single penny. Things everyone can take pleasure in, every single day, if only we paid just a little more attention to them. For me it's singing along with one of my favorite songs, the smell of rain, sunshine on my face, a hot cup of tea, sex, laughing so hard my belly hurts, a hot shower, dancing in the kitchen with my daughters, candlelight, birdsong, the smell of coffee, helping somebody, flowers in bloom, a walk, a hug. It's all pure bliss. Not a bucket list, not parties or material objects. No, it's all the mundane little things right under my nose. Actually, happiness is little more than being satisfied and content. Wanting what we already have. And the moment you realize that: gratitude.

*

One of the most important facts I remember from college is that our brain isn't designed to make us happy, but to help us survive. Which implies that we actively have to seek out happiness ourselves. It's totally normal to very quickly take things for granted once we have them. It's how we're hardwired. That rushed, anxious feeling and powerful drive happen to be part of my personality, and I used to have a hard time taking pleasure in my figurative 'vegetable garden' – since I'd already be busy and on to the next piece of land to sow more and different seeds – so I made a point of training myself to be actively thankful more often. Not because I felt bad, since I actually felt fine, but to experience happiness more fully. Possibly it was because I wasn't consciously being present, living in the now, and always racing on to the next project. And as a bit of an emotional flatliner, I never really experienced being completely at peace, or a fluttery sensation in my tummy, or smiling from head to toe.

Almost immediately after I graduated, I enrolled in Tony Robbins' training program for coaches. He taught me that humans are constantly on the lookout for danger, because our brain is strongly focused on making sure we don't die just because we do something stupid. Our brain is always looking for things that are awry or absent, or opinions that could affect us. It's why humans have two potentially very destructive basic emotions: fear and anger. Those two are often at the root of pivotal moments in friendships, in romantic relationships, in parenting, in careers, or just in happiness in general. When I think back to really shitty moments in my life, I was either angry or anxious. And that's exactly why it's so important to train your brain in gratitude. Make sure to carve out time – during a spontaneous walk or right in those moments when you're feeling angry or anxious – to consciously ask yourself: "What am I grateful for? Why am I grateful for that? To what do I owe these things? What ten things make me happiest of all? What brings a smile to my face? And why? What would I miss the most if those things weren't around anymore?"

"

I will let go of the
things I do *not* control.
I will focus on what I do
control. And ENJOY the
little things. I hold that
key. I have the POWER
OF CHOICE.

"

Tony Robbins says gratitude is the only antidote against everything that messes up our lives. Our brain is simply incapable of being angry and grateful at the same time. Just like it's impossible to simultaneously be anxious and thankful. It's why a grateful mindset is so important, because we can not only harness gratitude to feel happier, but also reframe it into something positive when we're distressed, afraid or annoyed. This knowledge helped me so much whenever I was upset and worried. Like those terrible, fearful moments when I started bleeding during my pregnancy, or when a family member needed major surgery. As soon as I detect those emotions, I now immediately and mindfully focus on something I'm very grateful for. And it doesn't matter if it's happening right then and there, or was ten years ago, because I instantly feel the stress and negativity slip away. I instantly feel I'm letting go. I can make that choice, which is an incredibly powerful feeling.

Feeling gratitude can be challenging because there's usually so much going on around us – both in a positive and negative sense – that happiness passes us by and we find ourselves thinking, "Why didn't I enjoy it more?" Please do make time for those conscious moments of really contemplating matters you feel grateful for, whether you're experiencing it right then and there or it's something you can recall in detail from years ago. And truly embrace *that* feeling. Trust me, it's great! That's what I do every day now, consciously and mindfully identifying things I'm grateful for. Not obsessively – not that I will sit down and write down a whole long list or anything – but when I go outside, I now almost automatically think: "Ohhhhh, what a lovely temperature," or: "Hey, I hear birds!" or: "Oh yummy, already looking forward to the cup of coffee at work later." Years ago, this was something I was oblivious to, but noticing these things has really enriched my life. There's so much more to enjoy. So much more to be happy about. Simply by being more aware of all the wonderful little moments throughout the day. It's nothing short of a gift to know how to *not* get carried away by negativity and stress, but to be able to make time for happiness by being grateful every day. Jealousy and insecurity are the result of counting someone else's blessings instead of your own. Go count your own blessings every day and see what a difference it makes.

*

I'm a glass-half-full sort of person. I'm great at whining and griping, but funnily enough, it's not about the things that really matter, but about stupid, small stuff. And even then, I'm more joking around as a way to blow off steam than anything serious. I tend to downplay the big issues that do matter, however. It's because I don't want to get wrapped up in it. I'd much rather be happy. So I've chosen to stop focusing on what's lacking, or different than I would have preferred it to be. To stop caring about chasing towards more and more, or bigger or more exciting, more awesome. The questions I'd rather ask myself are: "What am I grateful for? What makes me happy? Suppose I knew tomorrow was my last day here, what would I do then?" *That's* what matters. Maybe being grateful has made me into the homebody I've become. Or maybe not, because I've always been that way, it's just that I've gotten so much better at knowing what makes me happy that I realize I'm not going to find it 'out there'. Because it's all here already, I don't have to go anywhere else for it.

After recovering from a serious illness, Dutch comedian Jochem Myjer once remarked: "That whole bucket list stuff doesn't go down well with me. When you hear you're going to die, it's not like, 'Oh wow, dammit, I would have loved to go bungee jumping over a volcano.' No, the first thing you think is, 'Shit, why did I work so hard?' The second thought is, 'If only I had spent more time with my family,' and the third, 'Why did I stay friends with that asshole for so long?' Those are the things you think about."

Yes, that's exactly my philosophy of life! I don't have a bucket list. Of course I want to have lots of fun, but I've realized it's actually the little things I most look forward to. Like spending time with my family. I will find myself thinking, "Oh yippee! I can take the girls to the playground this afternoon." Or: "Can't wait! My parents are coming over later, and are bringing pie from my hometown." Spending time with the people I love, enjoying things together, but also being by myself during those little in-between moments – it's pure bliss. And it's exactly what Jochem Myjer meant. Because sure, working is hard is great; you get things done. Yup, definitely! But in the end, what does all that hard work bring you? Everything we do takes up time. The big question is, what do you want to do with your precious time? What do you want to spend it on? Well, I've decided it's not going to be working even longer hours to be able to buy stuff which isn't going to make me happy anyway. Oh, and not on stupid asshole so-called friends either!

In love, I have chosen for what makes me happy. In friendships, I have chosen for happiness. And as a mother I organize things in such a way that it makes me happy. I now use my ambition for matters that fulfill me. And no, I didn't make all those choices simultaneously; it was a step-by-step process. I keep aiming to create happiness for myself, and to really notice it and take pleasure in it. To be content with it and to absorb it. Like a nice walk with the girls and the dog. For me that's what true happiness is – in the forest, with my kids, the dog and my mom. To do something for someone else every day, whether that person realizes it or not, since that brings me joy. I would like to emphasize that I'm well aware that doing these completely 'normal' things are all moments where you have to make a choice, since there will be other matters clamoring for attention. This is still a challenge for me as well. To make sure I ask myself often enough, "What is really important to me right now? And am I focusing enough on those matters?"

Sometimes the trick is to be satisfied with where your life is at, without wanting more at all costs. My biggest achievements all concern my private life. My heart's desire has always been to have my own happy family. Having my own home, and having that be my favorite place. I have that now, so that's already the greatest success in my life. My companies have also been a success; as a working mother, I am managing to run them really well, and they have grown substantially too. And no, it definitely didn't just fall into my lap, but it's all worked out very well and I'm proud of that. What we say yes to and what we choose to decline informs our choices. It's how we start investing our time in the right things. In the people, matters and moments that actually make life more fun and joyous.

It makes me think of something Olympic medalist Bibian Mentel said before she died, and something I've also heard from other people facing a life-threatening disease. What they all said was: "Yes, sure, our life and our experiences were incredibly special – but you really learn to appreciate life when you're able to go to the playground with your kids and can sit there in the sun and watch them play. Those are the moments that really matter. Collect memories instead of things." Since I've made it a daily practice to identify what I'm grateful for, I'm noticing those things more. It helps me not to get too caught up in mundane stuff and forget to enjoy what I already have.

*

As a mother of small children, I'm able to look at the world through their eyes and be filled with wonder again about all kinds of little things. And I love that. The moments themselves, living in the now, and being able to enjoy that. I did really have to learn that, though. It's been a whole growth process, but I'm now at a point that on a wonderful fall day, I enjoy being able to close my laptop a bit earlier to go to the park and feed the ducks with the girls. There's usually an older couple there, sitting on a bench. Totally content together. Maybe that's the ultimate goal, to not have to *do* anything anymore, and just be. And being perfectly content and happy with that. I'd hate it if I would have to wait until I'm 80 years old to be able to experience that, however. Why not now?

I'm grateful for the solid foundation my childhood home afforded me, whether it's due to my genes or all the experiences and lessons. The ups and downs in self-esteem, self-love and love, friendship, motherhood, ambition and loss have made me who I am today. I wouldn't want to be anyone else anymore, which feels wonderful. Many people say say, "She's done well for herself!" when they look at me. And they're probably right, but what also played a major role is that so many things *didn't* work out. Because I dared to choose, and wanted to find out what different choices would result in. Whether it would make me happy. Because if there's one thing I've always been lucky in, it's the confidence that everything would turn out fine in the end. Is a relationship not working out? I'll find someone else. Is a friend no longer a good match for me? Some other friendship will be sure to come along. Is my company heading downhill? I'll find myself another job.

Whatever happens, it's always better than the nagging feeling of "If only I had...", which torments so many people – temporarily, and sometimes their whole life. It's often better to regret something you *did* do than what you didn't. To avoid wondering what would have happened if you had dared to take that step. And of course there's a difference between a rash decision and an informed choice. In the case of a very big step, I'd opt for the latter. Think it over carefully, and only then take action. And how do you know you've thought it through well enough? When you've asked yourself the right questions. When you've used the criteria of staying true to yourself and choosing for your own happiness. I'm grateful for having the power of choice, and I'm damn well going to use it too!

66

HAPPINESS
is *wanting* what you
already have!

99

ACKNOWLEDGEMENTS

Thank you, life, for all the ups and downs, which made me resilient and grateful.

Thank you to everyone who made my life a little more difficult, including myself; it made me stronger and wiser.

Thank you to everyone who made my life a little easier; without you this book would not have existed.

Thank you to all my readers; without you there wouldn't even have been a series, and every day it's still so incredible to receive all kinds of sweet messages about the wonderful things my words have brought you. I will never take that for granted.

Thank you to everyone who is so very, very dear to me; the fact that all the choices I made have led me to this point here and now, with you, is my greatest source of happiness. I would choose you guys again any day, any time.

Thank you to myself; trial and error sure gets you somewhere, right? I'm so proud you keep on putting your back into it and keep trying your very best to make you and the people around you happy.

FURTHER READING

Inspiration for this book came from my college years, from postgraduate courses, from lectures by peers, from my own companies, and from the thousands of people I was fortunate enough to coach, plus all the inspiring life stories I hear every day, directly and indirectly, online and offline.

The following is a list of the main books I consulted:

American Psychiatric Association (2013). *Diagnostic and Statistical Manual of Mental Disorders*

Baer, R. A. (2014). *Geluk betrachten* (Dutch translation of *Practicing Happiness*). Nieuwezijds B.V.

Beck, J. S. (1999). *Cognitieve gedragstherapie: theorie en praktijk* (Dutch translation of *Cognitive Behavior Therapy: Basics and beyond*). HB Uitgevers

Chapman, G. (2019). *De vijf talen van de liefde* (Dutch translation of *The Five Love Languages*). Ark Media

Cranenburgh, B. (2009). *Neurowetenschappen: Een overzicht* ("Neuroscience: An Overview.") Reed Business

Davey, G. (2014). *Psychopathology: Research, Assessment and Treatment in Clinical Psychology.* Chichester: BPS Blackwell

De Hond, M. (2020). *Licht in de tunnel* ("Light in the tunnel"). Lev.

Frankl, V.E. (2008). *Man's Search for Meaning.* Beacon Press

Gray, P. (2010). *Psychology.* Worth Publishers U.S.

Hengeveld, M.W. & Schudel, W.J. (2003 or a later edition). *Het psychiatrisch onderzoek* ("Psychiatric examination"). Wetenschappelijke Uitgeverij Bunge

Gawdat, M. (2017). *De logica van geluk* (Dutch translation of *Solve for Happy*). Uitgeverij Brandt

Kabat-Zinn, J. (2013). *Mindfulness voor beginners* (Dutch translation of *Mindfulness for Beginners*). Nieuwezijds B.V.

Manson, M. (2016). *The Subtle Art of Not Giving a F*ck: a Counterintuitive Approach to Living a Good Life.* HarperOne

Mentel, B. (2021). *LEEF* ("LIVE"). Splint Media B.V.

Nolen-Hoeksema, S. (2012 or a later edition).
    Abnormal Psychology. McGraw-Hill
Rigter, J. (2008). *Het palet van de psychologie*
    ("The palette of psychology"). Coutinho
Sinek, S. (2011). *Start with Why*. Penguin Books Ltd.
Vandereyken W., Hoogduin, C.A.L. &
    Emmelkamp, P.M.G. (2000 or a later edition).
    Handboek psychopathologie ("Handbook
    Psychopathology") Bohn Stafleu van Loghum